Door of Hope Ministries Presents

A Kingdom Revolution

Birthing the True Sons of God in the Earth

Author: Minister Bonjie Wernecke Rodriguez

Door of Hope Ministries Presents

A Kingdom Revolution

Birthing the True Sons of God in the Earth

Author: Minister Bonjie Wernecke Rodriguez

Unless otherwise indicated, all Scripture quotations are taken from the New American Standard Version of the Bible.

The author has emphasized some words in Scripture quotations in italicized type.

A Kingdom Revolution

Birthing the True Sons of God in the Earth

ISBN 13:9798749383089

ISBN 10:9798749383089

PO Box 781, Deer Park, TX 77536

www.mydoorofhopeministries.org

Contents

Introduction

Birthing the True Sons of God in the Earth

This message was born out of something that God spoke to me. One night, I couldn't sleep so I went to the kitchen to get a light snack. While standing there, without anything spiritual on my mind- I heard the Lord say, "The British are coming, The British are coming!" The more I pondered this, the more I realized that the Lord was giving me a prophetic message.

As I thought about the statement, "The British are coming", the Lord began to give me a prophetic download about what's on the horizon in America. Since this is the way God often speaks to me, I knew it was time to go study and pray it through until completion.

Over 200 years ago, a man by the name of Paul Revere sounded an alarm; saying: "The British Are Coming!" This was an alarm prompting the colonists to arise and confront tyranny by proclaiming, "The British Are Coming!" As others struggled, he took stock of the situation around him and sensed that his own livelihood could soon be affected, unless the issues with the British were soon addressed.

During the war, Revere wore many different hats. They respected him for his work and he involved himself in the chaos that was bringing danger to those around him. The American colonists believed Britain was unfairly taxing them to pay for expenses incurred during the French and Indian War. American colonists, frustrated and angry at Britain for imposing "taxation without representation," dumped 342 chests of tea, imported by the British into the Boston Harbor. In simplest terms, the Boston Tea Party happened as a result of 'this taxation', yet the cause is more complex than that. As tensions between the colonies and the British deepened, in a brazen act of defiance Paul Revere and others dressed as Indians to spy on British soldiers and report on their movement.

As recorded in History; On April 18, 1775, at ten' o'clock that night, Revere rode to Lexington to warn John Hancock and Samuel Adams of the approaching British. It was his ride that etched his name into history. With this warning, came the war or what we know to be the American Revolution.

As we begin to scan our worldview in the earth TODAY, we see similarity of the American Revolution War. We know there are many kinds of wars. There are civil, government, religious, and yet we know the highest of all wars is 'SPIRITUAL WARS.'

The Apostle Paul wrote, "For the weapons of our warfare are not carnal but mighty through God to the pulling down of strongholds" (2 Corinthians 10:4). Strongholds are fortified belief systems known as kingdoms. We know more than ever, especially if you watch the media, and the White House, Christians are in a spiritual war for freedom. Evil spirits are attacking our Christian beliefs and values on every side of these spiritual wars. We see kingdom against kingdom, culture against culture, values against values, truth against lies, and seductions, man-made false beliefs and light against darkness through worldwide views. They pass through the hierarchy from men to men that in turn will be passed to others. But the truth of the matter is when we pull back the curtain, we understand the true warfare is the battle against God and His Kingdom fueled by the hatred of Satan and his kingdom.

Yet similar to the AMERICAN REVOLUTION; God wants to start a KINGDOM REVOLUTION in our life. There are so many in the Body of Christ, who have just given up, and they're not believing for a breakthrough—or they are just waiting for it to fall in their lap. We think we're waiting on God, but really, He's waiting on us to finish our end of obedience. When we get serious about making the necessary adjustments in our life, then we're preparing a place for God to manifest HIS KINGDOM GLORY!

We hear a lot about reformation and revolution. What is the difference between the two? A REFORMATION improves the status quo, but a REVOLUTIONIST overthrows the status quo. Reformers gradually bring change by modifying the status quo in new ways; but a revolutionist disrupts and overthrows status quo never to return to the old way of thinking. THAT IS WHAT WE MEAN BY A KINGDOM REVOLUTION. A KINGDOM REVOLUTION means a forcible overthrow of an OLD WAY OF THINKING INTO A BRAND-NEW WAY. Therefore, as we stand in our kingdom liberty, we are a part of that KINGDOM REVOLUTION that never returns to the 'OLD WAY OF THINKING' but allows the Spirit of God to completely revolutionize us!

Isaiah 43: 18-19 says, "Do not call to mind the former things, or ponder things of the past. Behold, I will do something new, Now it will spring forth; Will you not be aware of it? I will even make a roadway in the wilderness, rivers in the desert."

As a believer in Christ, you are part of that KINGDOM REVOLUTION that never returns to the 'OLD YOU' but allows the Spirit of God to completely 'REVOLUTIONIZE' you! Without Christ, none can be free and without His overcoming resurrection power to break the chains of tyranny, none of us could be liberated. THEREFORE our hope is completely in Him, and Him alone.

You may even wonder how does this apply to you today? Which brings me to the reason for writing this book. Hidden in the pages of this BOOK you will see the unfolding of a KINGDOM REVOLUTION: BIRTHING THE TRUE SONS OF GOD IN THE EARTH; and guess what? No man will take credit for this KINGDOM REVOLUTION because it's ALL GOD AND NOT MAN'S ACCOMPLISHMENT.

Part 1

A KINGDOM REVOLUTION

Birthing the True Sons of God in the Earth

God's Word says that all creation is groaning as it waits for the revealing of the TRUE Sons of God. This is a pivotal time for the Sons of God to manifest and be awakened in their purpose. Sonship is so important that all creation is presently crying out for the manifestation of the mature sons of God.

Romans 8:14-25 declares: "For all who are being led by the Spirit of God, these are sons of God. For you have not received a spirit of slavery leading to fear again, but you have received a spirit of adoption as sons by which we cry out, "Abba! Father!" The Spirit Himself testifies with our spirit that we are children of God, and if children, heirs also, heirs of God and fellow heirs with Christ, if indeed we suffer with Him so that we may also be glorified with Him. For I consider that the sufferings of this present time are not worthy to be compared with the glory that is to be revealed to us. For the anxious longing of the creation waits eagerly for the revealing of the sons of God. For the creation was subjected to futility, not willingly, but because of Him who subjected it, in hope that the creation itself also will be set free from its slavery to corruption into the freedom of the glory of the children of God. For we know that the whole creation groans and suffers the pains of childbirth together until now. And not only this but also, we ourselves, having the first fruits of the Spirit, even we ourselves groan within ourselves, waiting eagerly for our adoption as sons, the redemption of our body."

We are living in an exciting time where we will see the greatest restoration take place in the body of Christ. God is doing this so that we can walk in the full expression of what He has released on the earth today. God is bringing us into a greater intensity because He is taking the church into a higher level of warfare, requiring us to understand greater mysteries we've never understood before.

Jesus often taught in parables to make a truth more engaging to those who were in a relationship with Him. This is a very important truth for us, that we shouldn't share intimate secrets with just anybody. God wants to show us heavenly mysteries of the kingdom, but those mysteries are only revealed to those who will hunger for an intimate and personal encounter with the Lord.

The disciples ask a poignant question to Jesus in the gospels. They ask, "Why do you speak to the people in parables?" Jesus replies to them, "The knowledge of the secrets of Heaven has been given to you, but not to them." He says, "This is why I speak to them in parables: Though seeing they do not see, though hearing, they do not hear or understand." (Mark 4:11-13) From this text, we understand that Jesus only taught mysteries to those who will go deeper and higher with Him.

And even when we're not spiritually mature; we still can't understand the deeper teachings of Christ, until we're ready. Paul said to the Corinthians saying, "I could not address you as spiritual, but as carnal-mere infants in Christ. I gave you milk, not solid food, for you were not ready for it." (1 Corinthians 3:1-3) This group of believers were saved, but they still followed their carnal mind because they were still infants. Thus, they could not see nor hear as the mature followers of Christ could.

Yet through time each one of us are being developed spiritually; and as we walk through those stages we must listen through personal encounters to the Lord to hear new mysteries where we draw strength and fortitude for the battle. Jeremiah 33:3 says, "Call unto Me and I will answer you, and I will show you great and mighty things, which you do not know." The Hebrew word for 'mighty' means 'mysteries or deep hidden intimate secrets.'

Then Proverbs 25:2 says, "It's the glory of God to conceal a matter, but the glory of a king to search it out." This reveals that the Lord Himself reveals secrets to those whom He trusts. Once understood and revealed, those that are carrying the secrets of the Kingdom have a mandate to steward it well and to reveal it to others in their proper time. We have an example of this in Ephesians 3:3-6 (NASB) as Paul, the Apostle stated, "How that by revelation there was made known to me (Paul) the mystery; (as I wrote before briefly by referring to this, when you read you can understand my insight into the mystery of Christ) which in other generations was not made known to mankind, as it has now been revealed to His holy apostles and prophets in the Spirit; to be specific, that the Gentiles are fellow heirs and fellow members of the body, and fellow partakers of the promise in Christ Jesus through the gospel."

Discernment allows a person to know the timing of God's release. We know that there were some who Jesus revealed His secrets to — those who were closest to Him, His Apostles and Prophets and His disciples. He trusted them on an intimate level to be obedient to the will of God, and He knew they had the understanding to carry forth His plans on the earth. Before they crucified Jesus, He prays for two groups of believers. In one prayer, Jesus prays for His disciples (the mature ones) and in another, He prays for all believers. Therefore, we see the difference here; it is simply a fact that the Lord reveals His secrets to those He entrusted to deliver the message to the people.

There are those who are simply not ready to receive the mysteries of the Kingdom of God. However, the Father prepares us through different stages of our maturity to understand the mysteries of Christ, and to show His Kingdom in and through us as the sons of God.

While some men (speaking of gender) may find this hard to accept; in the spiritual realm, we are pregnant with God's purpose; which applies to both men and women. Sonship isn't about gender, but spiritually God has impregnated every one of us in the realm of the Spirit with the Seed of Faith in the Son of God. When we become born again, the Holy Spirit deposits THE SEED in each of our lives, and progressively the Spirit of God is nurturing us as we grow and develop into maturity on the inside of our spirit man. As Jesus grows and matures on the inside of us, the stretching, the discomfort, and even the spiritual mood swings seem to continue to get worse and worse to accelerate God's purpose. The Holy Spirit is making room in our inner man for His Kingdom to come forth in us! While the stretching process is extremely uncomfortable in the spiritual realm; God is birthing something in and through our life. All of those times of intimacy, intercession and prayer (where you even feel like nothing is happening) are about to manifest. The Holy Spirit has been fashioning something powerful on the inside of you to bring you into God's plan. Galatians 4:19 (AMP) says, "My little children, for whom I am again suffering birth pangs until Christ is completely and permanently formed (molded) within you."

I love the tenderness that the Apostle Paul reveals in scripture where he speaks of his travail toward his spiritual children like child birth on their behalf until it forms Christ in them. We are all in the process of having Christ completely molded within as we're all being conformed into His image day by day, into the image of God's beloved Son. Romans 8: 29 (WEB) Paul writes "... For whom He foreknew, He also predestined to be conformed to the image of His Son, that He might be the firstborn among many brothers."

The Word of God is growing within you the Seed of Resurrection Power to bring you into full spiritual maturity. Colossians 1:27 (NASB) says, "...to whom God willed to make known what the wealth of the glory of this mystery among the Gentiles is, the mystery that Christ in you, the hope of glory." Whatever the Holy Spirit causes you to birth; you'll be filled with God's glory; and as it comes forth it won't just resemble you, but it will resemble our beloved King who placed it inside of you. Having said that;

let's continue with understanding what God is doing in the earth.

The Lord has continuously given me a download about where we are prophetically in the plan of God. We truly are at a place in time where God is revealing deep hidden mysteries to His Body. I truly believe that we are in a season where the Lord is bringing His order to the heart of the Church.

There are major changes taking place on the horizon. The true sons of God are experiencing a great awakening that will overthrow a man made government and bring us under another government called The Kingdom of God. This will bring about a significant paradigm shift from the current normal or status quo into the Kingdom of God.

Unfortunately, many do not get what A KINGDOM REVOLUTION represents. It's certainly not a "churchy mindset." Many find the spiritual authority and governing influence of the TRUE SONS OF GOD a **foreign concept**. When Christ announced the Kingdom of God, He was referring to the restoration of the rule of Christ in the earth through His body, representing the true sons of God bringing restoration. The true sons of God have a HIGH CALLING to announce and launch a kingdom revolution movement that turned the world upside down. Therefore, we can see the pattern for kingdom restoration and a governing influence even in the Old Testament. Scripture says, "Then said Samuel to the people, Come, and let us go to Gilgal and renew (which means restore) the kingdom there. And all the people went to Gilgal and there they made Saul king before the LORD in Gilgal" (1 Samuel 11:14-15). Saul responded with a mindset of an organized man centered way. The traditional organized church is just like Saul where they think the same old man-centered way of doing church over and over every time they meet, with self- absorbed methods, yet they have no power to stand against the enemy.

Even though the people made a wrong choice of a leader, God was still activating the KINGDOM OF GOD in the earth. Sounds familiar doesn't it as we look at our government today. But we're not doomed just because a wrong leader is in position. This was demonstrated in Gilgal even after Saul was in leadership; yet through a governing people who were in one accord with God's purpose; and with it came the restoration of the kingdom.

The ministry of Christ isn't finished yet, and it is going to come forth in great glory and power. 1 Corinthians 15:24-28 says, "... then comes the end, when He hands over the kingdom to God the Father, when He has abolished all rule and all authority and power. For He must reign until He has put all His enemies under His feet." When the scripture says, "All things are put in subjection under His feet," it means that the Son Himself subjected all things to God, the Father, so that God may exalt His kingdom in us.

The enemy truly is under our feet because Jesus put him there. Ephesians 1:22 says, "And He (Jesus) put all things in subjection under His feet, and gave Him as head over all things to the church." The Holy Spirit is still decreeing restoration today through a people as it says in Acts 3: 19-21, "Therefore repent and return, so that your sins may be wiped away, in order that times of refreshing may come from the presence of the Lord; and that He may send Jesus, the Christ appointed for you, whom heaven must receive until the period of the restoration of all things, about which

God spoke by the mouths of His holy prophets from ancient times."

Kingdom restoration began long ago in the heart of God. This was not a part of God's plan, IT WAS THEN AND STILL IS HIS PLAN TODAY TO BRING A KINGDOM REVOLUTION THROUGH THE SONS OF GOD.

Throughout the scriptures we find the meaning of a KINGDOM REVOLUTION. Therefore, the unity of the faith is not found in methods but in unity of purpose. Methods will not change the world or the way we do church as usual. Unity of methods is not what the Apostle Paul was referring to in the scriptures. (Ephesians 4:11-16)

These same leaders that are thrilled when hundreds get saved will break fellowship with each other over such things such as speaking in tongues, the reality of deliverance, the method of water baptism, or how often one takes communion. It's ridiculous what they split hairs over. The unity of the faith is not found in Christian methods of 'the way we're doing church' but in reality the unity of the faith is when the True Sons of God come together to restore the Kingdom of God in the earth through the revelation of Christ being manifested through us. Once we understand we are under the rule and influence of the LORD, as His royal priesthood, we will become what we see Him as. Yet if our eyes are on the kingdoms of this world, we can become seduced and ruled by another realm.

We must understand there are two systems: One is the system of the world and the other is the Kingdom of God. Jesus said, "My kingdom is not of this world. If My kingdom were of this world (cosmos), then My servants would be fighting so that I would not be handed over to the Jews; but as it is, My kingdom is not of this realm." (John 18:36)

The word 'world' in the Greek is 'cosmos.' Jesus was saying, "My authority is not of human origin, because I operate through a different Kingdom." Jesus then told us what His mission was. He said, "You say correctly that I am a king. For this, I have been born, and for this, I have come into the world, to testify to the truth. Everyone who is of the truth hears My voice." (John 18:37) Then Jesus said in Luke 6: 46, "Why do you call Me, 'Lord, Lord,' and do not do what I say?" The word 'Lord' suggests a close relationship.

'Lord' means to be supreme, and it implies submission to His authority. The meaning of 'Adonai', which is the Hebrew word for 'Lord', means is to give Him first place or preeminence in our life. In Greek, the word for 'Lord' is 'Kurios' and it means 'to govern'. Then as we put these two meanings together, it means as we give Jesus first place in our life, we will govern through a priestly and kingly anointing. That's how the kingdom operates because it's within us.

Jesus said, "... for the kingdom of God is not eating and drinking, but righteousness and peace and joy in the Holy Spirit." (Romans 14:17) The kingdom is released through us as believers, which changes the surrounding environment in the earth.

Therefore, understanding "the earth is the Lord's and the fullness thereof" brings substance to the restoration (or the renewal) of the Kingdom of God. The word 'kingdom' suggests a people who are governed by a king. The word 'KINGDOM' contains two words, 'king' and 'dom.' It indicates a domain that has a king ruling over and through our lives. The Kingdom of God has a purpose for us to fulfill, and that purpose represents releasing God's purpose into the earth. Revelation 1: 6 says "We are a KINGDOM OF PRIESTS UNTO GOD." This also confirms that when God created the heavens and the earth; He gave us dominion to rule like Adam was supposed to in the garden, but he committed treason and surrendered his kingship to the serpent (the devil).

However, Jesus redeemed us back and gave it to the true sons of God to rule and reign with Him in heavenly places. Ephesians 2: 4b-6 says, "But God being rich in mercy, because of His great love with which He loved us, even when we were dead in our wrongdoings, made us alive together with Christ (by grace you have been saved), and raised us up with Him and seated us with Him in the heavenly places in Christ Jesus."

In the days ahead of us, this is the season of light, the season of transition, the season of elevation, and the season in which we will have an opportunity to SHIFT AND go higher than we've ever been before.

Therefore, the framework of our journey will determine how we receive the blessings that God has in store for His people. I cannot emphasize enough how vital it is that we position ourself correctly regarding how God is leading His people. This hour is so pivotal that God is establishing, that we must stay focused AND GO DEEPER INTO HIS HEART and get to know Him with greater depth. This truly is a new beginning, but the enemy is going to do whatever he can to cause us to MISS THE IMPORTANT POINT.

That is why we must run the race that is set before us with endurance and seek God's wisdom to stay on the right track, because circumstances will arise that have the potential of getting us sidetracked. Deuteronomy 5:32 says, "Therefore you shall be careful to do as the LORD your God has commanded you; you shall not turn aside to the right hand or to the left."

Then Hebrews 12:1 says, "Therefore we also, since we are surrounded by so great a cloud of witnesses, let us lay aside every weight, and the sin which so easily ensnares us, and let us run with endurance the race that is set before us..." Therefore let me encourage you as well as myself to stay focused on the Lord.

The Apostle Peter taught about a kingdom mindset as well. 1 Peter 2:9 says, "But you are a chosen generation, a royal priesthood, a holy nation, a peculiar people; that you should show forth the praises of Him who has called you out of darkness into his marvelous light." Therefore, let's receive what rightfully belongs to us as the true sons of God. It's time to let go of things that tie us to the past, so we can move forward in God's purposes. We're moving into a place of great liberty and fullness than we have ever known before.

Chapter 1

THE ORPHAN MINDSET

Birthing the True Sons of God in the Earth

There's a great awakening happening in the earth today, however, before we can see this great awakening unfold, we must overcome the orphan mindset. You may wonder, "What is an Orphan mindset?" Romans 8:14-25 declares: "For all who are being led by the Spirit of God, these are sons of God. For you have not received a spirit of slavery leading to fear again, but you have received a spirit of adoption as sons by which we cry out, "Abba! Father!" The Spirit Himself testifies with our spirit that we are children of God..."

Orphans do not comprehend their identity as "the sons of God" because they do not walk in the Spirit; but instead they are led by their emotions and a wounded spirit that's held them hostage to painful memories. Therefore, the orphan mindset is enslaved to working for love and is opposite to how God thinks and how His Kingdom is set up. Many people have been wounded in the church and have wandered away from their spiritual inheritance. They've wandered away because someone who was an authoritative figure in their life hurt them. This hurt sent them looking for affirmation and self-worth, but unfortunately in all the wrong places.

To make matters worse, in our contemporary society, with the breakup of the nuclear family, large amounts of people are not only alienated from God but are raised without the love, care and security of their biological fathers. Presently, millions of incarcerated men and women are acting out of violence and rebellion because their earthly fathers wounded and abandoned them.

Orphaned men have a hard time connecting to their spouses, children, spiritual fathers, and any natural or spiritual authority. They also have a hard time accepting and loving themselves. The enemy knows if he can wound us early on; he can damage our identity through hurt and wounds that will hinder our destiny.

An orphan mindset is a person who lacks spiritual and emotional identity and seeks to earn his identity through his or her own efforts. Their symptoms include a critical spirit, being defensive, unable to take correction, feeling abandoned, seeking for approval and blaming others.

The story of the prodigal son (Luke 15:11-32) is the story of two sons with an orphan mindset. The younger son spends his inheritance in pursuit of pleasure. The older son works to earn his father's love, not realizing he already had his father's love and favor. The younger son represents people who run from Father God believing that they don't need Him, and the older son represents many people in the church who believe they are close to Father God through religious works but in reality they do not know the Father's love. Both sons live as orphans with a poverty spirit. The younger son finally realizes the error of his ways, but the older son continues to earn his father's love, favor and acceptance through self-righteous religious works.

The Church & the Orphan Mindset

And unfortunately, the orphan mindset is alive and well TODAY. The church has lived with the ORPHAN MINDSET for so long that the supernatural cannot manifest because of their fear of failure, chronic dishonor toward spiritual fathers that have wounded them, and disappointment toward God. They feel disconnected from the Father's love, leaving them with feelings of being orphaned; always feeling like they are on the outside looking in, but never feeling like a part of the family. God's church should be a place that offers them acceptance and grace because that's what Jesus offered us in the Beloved. Ephesians 1:6-12 says, "...to the praise of His glorious grace, which He has freely given us in the one He loves. In Him we have redemption through His blood, the forgiveness of sins, in accordance with the riches of God's grace that He lavished on us. With all wisdom and understanding, He made known to us the mystery of His will according to His good pleasure, which He purposed in Christ, to be put into effect when the times reach their fulfillment—to bring unity to all things in heaven and in earth under Christ. In Him we were chosen, having been predestined according to the plan of Him who works out everything in conformity with the purpose of His will, in order that we, who were the first to put our hope in Christ, might be for the praise of His glory."

As the church, we really don't understand the power of grace. Jesus said, in John 14:18-20, 23 "I will not leave you as orphans; I will come to you. After a little while the world will see Me no more, but you will see Me; because I live, you will live also. In that day you will know that I am in my Father and you in Me, and I in you. If anyone loves Me, he will keep My Word; and My Father will love him, and we will come to him and make Our home with him."

When Jesus said the word 'home,' He was referring to a place of acceptance where we find rest and security in our identity in Him, where we never have to strive for acceptance. That's why He gives us grace. Grace means that God takes all our mistakes and causes them to serve an ETERNAL PURPOSE INSTEAD OF SERVING SHAME. That eternal purpose brings transformation; transforming us from orphans into warrior kings who rule and reign with Jesus in heavenly places. (Ephesians 2:6)

The scriptures reveal how Jesus was empowered through the blessing of His father's love that was mantled on Him through the affirmation of His Father. As Jesus stood in the Jordan River to be baptized by John the Baptist, he heard His Father affirm Him saying, "This is my BELOVED SON in whom I am well pleased." (Matthew 3:13)

Jesus had a tight bond with His Father. John 5:19 says, Therefore Jesus answered and was saying to them, "Truly, truly, I say to you, the Son can do nothing of Himself, unless it is something He sees the Father doing; for whatever the Father does, these things the Son also does in the same way."

Sonship is not About Gender

God has made it possible for the sons of God to be empowered through ruling and reigning with Him through Son-ship. Son-ship in God's Word is not about gender, but positionally taking our place with Him. As sons in God's family, we've been adopted, making us co-heirs with JESUS. The term 'heirs' of God emphasizes our relationship to God, the Father. The Greek term 'co-heirs' in Romans 8:17 refers to "those who receive their allotted possession by right of Sonship." Because God has made us His children (John 1:12), we have full rights to receive His inheritance. As His children, we have an inheritance that can never perish, spoil, or fade away. (1Peter 1:4)

As stated previously, to get it deep in our spirits Romans 8.15 -17 says, "For you did not receive the spirit of slavery to fall back into fear, but you have received the Spirit of adoption as sons, by whom we cry, "Abba! Father!" The Spirit Himself bears witness with our spirit that we are children of God, and if children, then heirs—heirs of God and joint heirs with Christ..."

The ancient Hebrew concept of adoption differs greatly from our western concept of adoption. The Hebrews adopted adult children. They were not looking for babies who were helpless and left without parents. The Hebrews were looking for mature young men who usually had two living parents, but couldn't raise them. An adopted son would have all the rights as a child born in a family; who would inherit their new adoptive father's identity, social standing, favor, wealth and power.

Therefore, God has a Hebrew understanding of adoption, and as stated, not a western concept. When God adopts us, He breaks off the orphan mindset and brings us into a new identity known as Sonship. Ephesians 1: 5 states, "He predestined us for adoption as sons through Jesus Christ, according to the purpose of His will..."

Only Almighty God Can Give US Our Self- Worth

Too many Christians have been brainwashed from the pulpit of religious preaching on how unworthy they are. Jesus didn't die to put shame on us, but to remove it off of us. How sad, that so many Christians do not understand the unlimited resources from a kingdom perspective that we have everything we need to live as Sons of the Most High God.

Those who have an orphan mindset are always trying to fill a GOD size hole that's in their soul by medicating their pain with things like alcohol, drugs, sex, food, or relationships. They are trying to satisfy a deeper hunger and their need to be loved. God adopts us not because we are unworthy, but because we are worthy. (Ephesians 1: 3-14)

The TRUTH is we will ONLY be fulfilled when we get our self-worth from Almighty God who created us. Yet an orphan mindset craves the FATHER'S LOVE, as they are always looking for acceptance, affirmation, and identity. They want to be constantly valued and not just merely be recognized as servants of God.

The True NT Word for Orphans is Slaves

THE TRUE NEW TESTAMENT WORD for an ORPHAN MINSET is 'slave' and not 'a servant.' The Greek word for sons is 'uihos' which translates to 'legitimate offspring', and the Greek word for children means 'a slavery mindset'.

As sons, we've been empowered to live victoriously being an heir through our God given identity. Slaves don't know what their master is doing or wants to do; because they serve out of duty and obligation and are mentally slaves and not sons. John 15:15-16 says, "No longer do I call you slaves, for the slave does not know what his master is doing; but I have called you friends, because all things that I have heard from My Father I have made known to you. You did not choose Me but I chose you, and appointed you that you would go and bear fruit, and that your fruit would remain, so that whatever you ask of the Father in My name He may give to you." John 8:34-35 says, Jesus answered them, "Truly, truly, I say to you, everyone who commits sin is the slave of sin. The slave does not remain in the house forever; the son does remain forever."

Slaves are in bondage to sin and do not abide in the house of the Lord, but sons are the ones that abide in the house of the Lord. The orphan mindset is perhaps the greatest curse on the earth today. According to the book of Malachi, without this restoration of the fathering spirit, we are under a curse. Malachi 4:2-3,5-6 says, "But for you who fear My name, the sun of righteousness will rise with healing in its wings; and you will go forth and skip about like calves from the stall. You will tread down the wicked, for they will be ashes under the soles of your feet on the day which I am preparing, says the LORD of hosts. Behold, I am going to send you Elijah the prophet before the coming of the great and terrible day of the LORD. He will restore the hearts of the fathers to their children and the hearts of the children to their fathers, so that I will not come and smite the land with a curse."

The Father's blessings are there for us to inherit. But we must refuse to think like an orphan. We must stop seeing ourselves as less than or as disqualified. When we became born again; the cleansing of the blood of Calvary washed away all the guilt and shame. Our worth is not determined by our past or what we've done, good or bad. The Father loves us, warts and all.

Another area we battle with is comparing ourselves with others. Paul said this is not wise to compare ourselves with others. 2 Corinthians 10:12-18 says, "For we do not presume to rank or compare ourselves with some of those who commend themselves; but when they measure themselves by themselves and compare themselves with themselves, they have no understanding. But we will not boast beyond our measure, but within the measure of our domain which God assigned to us a measure, to reach even as far as you. For we are not overextending ourselves, as if we did not reach even as far as you, for we were the first to come even as far as you in the gospel of Christ; not boasting beyond our measure, that is, in other people's labors, but with the hope that as your faith grows, we will be within our domain, enlarged even more by you, so as to preach the gospel even to the regions beyond you and not to boast in what has been accomplished in the domain of another. But the one who boasts is to boast in the Lord. For it is not the one who commends himself that is approved, but the one whom the Lord commends."

We should never compare ourself to others or their accomplishments. We are incomparable. There is no legitimate comparison we can make by looking at what others are doing or what they have achieved in their life. If we're going to be authentic, we should be who God has called us to be, and see ourselves as He sees us.

Those around us may suggest we need to be like this person or that person, but we do not find our authenticity in thinking, talking or acting like another person we admire. It's fine to admire them and be encouraged by their faith, but get your instructions directly from God's heart. Many try to emulate and be like someone else, but what does that accomplish? There are no shortcuts to our destiny, therefore, when others offer you shortcuts, just realize they are merchandising you for their benefit and not your own.

God is your source of inspiration, truth and direction. Only Almighty God can give us our self- worth, which in turn will set us into our God- ordained purpose.

David was a man after God's own heart, but a man named Joab plagued him through his life. In Joab's eyes, they met David with scorn one day and flattery on another. The day came that Solomon succeeded and put Joab to death. Therefore, it's wise to cut off all such contaminated relationships with those people that you never know where you stand with them. Those who flatter you one day and scorn you the next; they will falsely claim they speak for God. However, we must look to God and allow Him to shape us in our calling; and that can only happen through relationship.

If we're going to step into our calling; we must first find out, "Is my authenticity based on a personal relationship to My Father?" If so; then God's purpose will be accomplished in your life, and His purpose will be made tangible through your identity. Therefore knowing our identity in the Lord will also cause us to walk in boldness. It will shift you into great places that He is leading you to. Proverbs 28:1 says, "The righteous are bold as a lion." Time and time again in the scriptures we see it repeatedly where God wants us to grow our faith into a God- confidence. Peter is one example. THE BOLDNESS OF GOD enabled PETER to say TO THE LAME MAN at the Gate Beautiful, "In the NAME OF JESUS CHRIST of

Nazareth, rise up and walk." (Acts 3:6) Peter spoke boldly in Jesus' Name because his identity was no longer rooted in insecurity. Peter said, "And through faith in HIS Name, this faith has made this man strong...." (Acts 3:16) All of Peter's insecurity left, when he allowed the boldness of God to take rule in his soul.

As we meditate on who the Word says we are, it will strike a death blow to insecurity. God longs to manifest the TRUE SONS OF GOD IN THE EARTH, but that can't happen until we allow the Spirit of God to transform our identity and draw us into true sonship.

We have the same Spirit in us that raised Christ from the dead. Yet do we believe that? Never forget the Father deeply loves us. We are not in competition with anyone for His love and care. We are a part of the body of Christ, just as significant as every other part of the body of Christ. We do not have to strive for significance. We are already significant. As we spend time delighting ourselves in the Father's love, it will set us free from the need to perform for anyone.

We shouldn't be living for the applause of anyone. Our father's approval is all we need. And He has already decided to love us even while we were yet sinners, Christ died for us. (Romans 5:8) The world is waiting on you true Sons of God to manifest in the earth. Now, go out and serve through the power of the Holy Spirit within you! This is so crucial; when you realize the power that resides within you, all those insecurities will leave as well.

The Lord is whispering to your heart, saying, "Your worth is determined by who I am in you and what I did for you on the cross. You have nothing to prove. The blood was enough, therefore, receive that cleansing blood and let the sacrifice of Calvary be enough for all your heart needs."

The Father longs to bring the spirit of Sonship into your identity so that you can inherit all the promises and blessings that He has ordained for you in Christ. Jesus Himself said, "I will not leave you as orphans!" (John 14:18) So kingdom inheritors, when are you going to get it? Forsake all orphan thinking through the power of the Holy Spirit, so that you can inherit all that God has the promised you in His kingdom.

Chapter 2

APOSTOLIC ORDER

Birthing the True Sons of God in the Earth

The blessings of our spiritual inheritance are ahead of us; but they are not just for us alone, but for all those who comprise our most intimate circle, our family, our tribe and our community. God is setting us up for a change, but we must unite corporately to get where God is leading. God knows we must unify and train for where He is taking us. Therefore, that means more transition is in the making because it's a part of life.

Father (Apostolic) & Mother (Prophetic) Training

The church needs fathering (Apostolic) and mothering (Prophetic) leadership or they will walk in an orphan mindset, and they will be under illegitimate authorities, which will cause all kinds of breaches, wounding and division. The greatest promises of God are just ahead, and as we embrace God's order, He will give us the revelations to walk out His original blueprint.

The Eagle Concept

Have you ever studied about Eagles and how the father & mother eagle prepare their little eaglets for life? Knowing nothing stays the same forever; the father and mother eagle will take the nest down where their little eaglets had all the comforts of their daily life to transition them into adulthood. The little eaglets are so comfortable in their daily routine, however, the father and mother eagles know they must prepare them for what's coming. Then suddenly, as their surroundings change; it causes them to be disoriented. They don't realize it, but the father and mother are shifting the atmosphere to EMPOWER them for their destiny.

Duet. 32:11-13 says, "Like an eagle that stirs up its nest, that hovers over its young, He spread His wings and caught them, He carried them on His pinions. The Lord alone guided him, and there was no foreign god with him. He made him ride on the high places of the earth..."

The Heavenly Eagle Nature

God is awakening the Eagles of this nation to arise into HIS PURPOSE. We need to be equipped like the

Eagle and keenly aware to do God's Apostolic Kingdom work. Therefore, it's crucial that we're alert and matured in our discernment. We've been awakened in this hour and God is gathering His people together to do great supernatural exploits. Daniel 11:32 IN THE LEB, says it this way, "Those who know their God will stand firm and will take firm action."

Eagles are so very majestic and they fly very swiftly, SOARING HIGH ABOVE THE TURBULENCE of the storm. THE EAGLE USED THEIR FEATHERS TO DETERMINE WHAT DIRECTION THEY SHOULD GO, in the turbulence similar to using the gift of DISCERNMENT.

The Lord is causing His people to be like the Eagle. He is causing us to ride high above the nations of the earth and overcome great adversity. We are being filled and flooded with God's presence as we set our attention on the Lord intentionally focusing on Him, and then we will fly into God's purpose and vision just like the eagle.

Yes; there is a heavenly nature on the inside of us that looks like an EAGLE, where we're being changed to look LIKE HIM. 2 Corinthians 3: 14 -17 says, "But their (the children of Israel) minds were hardened; for until this very day at the reading of the old covenant the same veil remains unlifted, because it is removed in Christ. But to this day whenever Moses is read, a veil lies over their heart; but whenever someone turns to the Lord, the veil is taken away. Now the Lord is the Spirit, and where the Spirit of the Lord is, there is freedom." THE ORIGINAL TEXT of this passage reads, "WHERE THE SPIRIT IS LORD, WE ARE LIBERATED." We are the image bearer of OUR Father, and WE ARE BEING BEAUTIFIED IN THE GLORY OF GOD WHO IS LIBERATING US to fly high into the purposes of God as we mount up on His Wings and we are strengthened day by day. Isaiah 40:31 says, (NRSB) "Those who wait for the Lord shall renew their strength, they shall mount up with wings like eagles, they shall run and not be weary; they shall walk and not faint."

Boundaries of Accountability

God has a principle in the Kingdom of God that many do not understand. Many do not know how to maintain healthy boundaries, therefore they take responsibility for areas that are not legitimately their issue. And the opposite is true when they transfer their rightful responsibility over to someone else. This causes more chaos and confusion in any situation.

One area that we often see in the Body of Christ, is the detrimental effects of a lack of not following concise boundaries. Even in the garden, God gave Adam and Eve boundaries of accountability. God told them to take dominion, subdue and cultivate the garden daily. He said you can eat of any tree in the garden except one. Yet they overstepped their responsibility and paid great consequences for their disobedient actions.

We shouldn't let people take advantage of us. When we let people walk all over us or we allow them to do just whatever they want, we are enabling the problem to get bigger. This really applies to every area of life; ministry, work, finances, health and relationships. Therefore, when we never let people pay the consequences for their actions, we're enabling them to never change. If we continue to rescue them for their inappropriate behavior, we are enabling the problem to go on, and usually it will get bigger, until we take proper action.

Our God-given authority is directly linked to owning what is our responsibility, and what is someone else's responsibility. We would do well to stay within the lines of our own jurisdiction and nothing more. We often think of boundaries of responsibility like fences on a property line that keep the good in and the bad out, creating a safety zone. Even God's Word says, "Don't be deceived, bad company corrupts good morals." (1 Corinthians 15:33) Therefore when we set healthy boundaries we're letting others know what is appropriate and what is not.

Keep Boundaries Firm

We could use so many unique examples in being good stewards; to keep our boundaries firm and knowing what's proper in many scenarios, but the bottom line is this; God intended for us to follow healthy boundaries in every area of our life and when we do; we will experience the true meaning of freedom.

With that in mind, boundaries draw a definitive line that gives everyone a proper understanding of what each of us are responsible for and what we are not;

and this is what gives us our freedom back. We must keep our boundaries firm, and this really operates in every area of our life. This is the beginning of true self-control. For example: If we're spending more than we have coming in, then we will pay the consequences if we get outside those financial boundaries.

If we don't live within healthy boundaries of getting a certain amount of rest, making good health choices and eating properly and drinking plenty of water and getting proper exercise for our bodies, then we will get outside of the boundaries that God intended, and we won't experience the blessing of good health.

The Apostolic Church Embodied in the Life of David

Now, let's look at examples of Apostolic Order as a biblical pattern in knowing healthy boundaries in God's Word. One thing we must clarify; The Apostolic Church is embodied in the life of David, where he served the purpose of God in his own generation. Acts 13:32-36 says, "And we preach to you the good news of the promise made to the fathers, that God has fulfilled this promise to our children in that He raised up Jesus. As it is also written in the second Psalm: You are My Son, today I have begotten You. As for the fact that He raised Him up from the dead, no longer to return to decay, He has spoken in this way: 'I will give you the holy and sure blessings of David.' Therefore He also says in another Psalm, 'You will not allow Your Holy One to undergo decay.' "For David, after he had served the purpose of God in his own generation, fell asleep, and was laid among his fathers and underwent decay; But He whom God raised did not undergo decay."

The Tabernacle of David's Restoration

Like David, and the Tabernacle of David, we have been designed to serve God's purpose in our generation as well. We've got to get rid of the "old church life" mentality and step into an apostolic move for the true biblical pattern of restoration to manifest.

You may wonder, "What is the tabernacle of David?" The Hebrew word for "tabernacle" is 'ohel', which means "a tent" or a covering, a dwelling place, home, tabernacle, or tent."

There are three primary references to the tabernacle (or tent) of David: Isaiah 16:5, Amos 9:11, and Acts

15:16-18 in which the Apostle James repeats the passage from both Acts and Amos. Both the Old and New Testament declare that the Tabernacle of David will be brought into restoration.

Acts 15:13-18 says, "After they stopped speaking, James responded, saying, "Brothers, listen to me. Simeon has described how God first concerned Himself about taking a people for His name from among the Gentiles." The words of the Prophets agree with this, just as it is written: "After this, I will return and will rebuild the tabernacle of David, which has fallen down; I will rebuild its ruins, and I will set it up. So that the rest of mankind may seek the Lord, even all the Gentiles who are called by My name, says the Lord who does all these things, known to God from eternity, are all His works."

Amos 9:11 says, "In that day I will raise up the fallen Tabernacle of David and wall up its breaches; I will also raise up its ruins and rebuild it as in the days of old."

And then specifically, the reference in Isaiah 16:5 refers to the tabernacle of David prophetically, pointing to One from the line of David who will someday sit on the throne and rule over all. This scripture reference is referring to Jesus.

Isaiah 16:5 says, "A throne will be established in faithfulness, and a judge will sit on it in trustworthiness in the tent of David. Moreover, He will seek justice and be prompt in righteousness."

God is setting everything back to HIS ORIGINAL BIBLICAL ORDER, to bring complete restoration. In the book of Ephesians, if we look at God's original blueprint; Paul lists the fivefold ministry gifts with the Apostle being listed first, then Prophet, Evangelist, Pastor and then Teacher. These spiritual gifts were given to the body of Christ to lead, govern and train the church for the work of the ministry.

Ephesians 4:11-13 says, "And He gave some as apostles, and some as prophets, and some as evangelists, and some as pastors and teachers, for the equipping of the saints for the work of service, to the building up of the body of Christ; until we all attain to the unity of the faith, and of the knowledge of the Son of God, to a mature man, to the full measure of the stature which belongs to the fullness of Christ."

This restoration can't happen until the Apostle is set back in their God ordained place as well. Matthew 20:16 says, "So the last shall be first, and the first last. For many are called, and few chosen."

What Does it mean to be Apostolic

Now, let's look at examples of Apostolic Order as a biblical pattern. When the church gets back to the original blueprint in God's Word, then the church will be brought back into restoration.

To put it simple, to be apostolic means to walk in the ways and teaching of Jesus the way the Apostles did in the book of Acts. In other words, they preached one message as their foundation. The results? Hundred, thousands and multitudes were added daily to the Kingdom of God.

- They were apostolic in the Word, devotion, fellowship and prayers. Together, the believers were united in harmonious fellowship with each other. All things were wrought by prayer and conquered with the power of the Word and the Spirit. Their doctrine was consistent and its power was pure and transforming. The Word of God was their foundation and the final authority. Acts 2:42 (KJV) says, "And they continued steadfastly in the apostles' doctrine and fellowship, and in breaking of bread, and in prayers.

- They were apostolic in identity. Untainted by the world. Though they lived in the world, they identified not with it. They identified themselves with the culture of the Kingdom of Christ, holy, set apart for His glory.

- They were apostolic in commitment. Everything they had belonged to the Lord. They lived in total abandonment to their Lord.

- They were apostolic in their giving. They gave sacrificially when they were instructed to.

- They were apostolic in their mission. Their mission was the world. They went where the Lord told them to go even when it meant their enemies and their greatest persecutors were there. Despite persecution, they didn't neglect meeting together.

- They were apostolic for the lost. They burned with a burden for the lost and a desire to see the whole world evangelized.

- They were apostolic in their worship. Their worship was extravagant and with utter obedience.

- They were apostolic in unity. Signs, miracles and wonders were performed and confirmed because of their unity. The church consisted of people belonging to different races and backgrounds and when brought together they had one quest – to seek His kingdom only! They were apostolic in working together as they equipped believers to do the work of the ministry.

- They were apostolic in moving in the gifts of the Spirit and used their gifts for the glory of God. They empowered every believer to offer their God-given gift in service to the Lord, and everyone was a minister.

- They were apostolic in being governed by the five-fold ascension gifts who were given to the church by Jesus Christ. The reason Ephesians 4:11 refers to the five fold as "ascension gift ministries," is because Jesus gave them when he ascended to the right hand of the Father.

- They were apostolic in demonstrating the power and the love of God. They lived with a passionate love for God and people.

The Apostolic Pattern

Using the example on a hand, the thumb, representing the apostle, touches all the offices of the fivefold ministry gifts to bring the restoration.

They are:

Apostle–**GOVERNS**- the thumb touches all the ministries.

Prophet–**GUIDES**-the pointer finger declares, "Thus saith the Lord."

Evangelist–**GATHERS SOULS**-the middle finger brings balance and reaches souls.

Pastor–**GUARDS**-the ring finger is married to the flock.

Teacher–**GROUNDS**- the little finger gets into places no one else can.

The Apostolic Pattern on the Hand

Therefore when we understand the apostolic pattern is like the order of the hand, it can't function without the thumb because the thumb touches all the other fingers and brings proper alignment and balance to all the hand needs to accomplish.

God's Governmental Order in His Ekklesia

David like JESUS represents a pattern of God's Governmental order sent to build His Ekklesia to bring it into complete restoration. We are not referring to a building but a God breathed organism that's been called out of this world to rule and reign with Jesus in heavenly places. (Ephesians 2:6)

One revelation that's being birthed through the true sons of God is knowing by the Spirit that Jesus is the patterned SON, that the Ekklesia is built on. Man won't build the Ekklesia, because Jesus will build it the way He wants it. Act 17:24 says, "The God who made the world and all things in it, since He is Lord of heaven and earth, does not dwell in temples made with hands".

The Greek word 'EKKLESIA' is a compound of two segments: 'ek', a meaning for 'out of' , and a verb, 'kaleo', signifying 'to call together', therefore literally Ekklesia means, 'to call out.' We need to be called out, and we will need a prophetic revelation of Jesus like Peter did in Matthew 16: 13-18. Peter received a prophetic revelation of Jesus that was astounding. When we read the account: Jesus confronted the disciples with a powerful question. The question was, "But who do you say that I am?" Simon Peter answered, "You are the Christ, the Son of the living God." In addition, Jesus said to him, "Blessed are you, Simon Barjona, because flesh and blood did not reveal this to you, but My Father who is in heaven. I also say to you that you are Peter, and upon this rock I will build My church; and the gates of Hades will not overpower it." (Matthew 16:13-18)

Jesus' response to Peter in Matthew 16, reveals that the Ekklesia is built on a prophetic revelation of JESUS CHRIST as an apostolic pattern and that's what the gates of Hell will not overpower. Peter saw a prophetic revelation of Jesus and the power that was connected to it. The Ekklesia IS NOT a building or a church, but a God-breathed organism that's built by the Spirit of God.

David's Apostolic Transition

David followed God's apostolic pattern bringing the Ark of God's presence into Jerusalem to bring governmental order in the land. 2 Samuel 6:2-11 says, "And David arose and went with all the people who were with him to Baale-Judah, to bring up from there the ark of God which is called by the Name, the very name of the LORD of hosts who is enthroned above the cherubim. They placed the ark of God on a **new cart** that they might bring it from the house of Abinadab, which was on the hill; and Uzzah and Ahio, the sons of Abinadab, were leading the **new cart**. So, they brought it with the ark of God from the house of Abinadab, which was on the hill; and Ahio was walking ahead of the ark. Meanwhile, David and all the house of Israel were celebrating before the LORD with all kinds of instruments made of fir wood, and with lyres, harps, tambourines, castanets and cymbals. But when they came to the threshing floor of Nacon, **Uzzah reached out toward the ark of God and took hold of it, for the oxen nearly upset it. And the anger of the LORD burned against Uzzah, and God struck him down there for his irreverence; and he died there by the ark of God.** David became angry because of the LORD'S outburst against Uzzah, and that place is called Perez-Uzzah to this day. So, David was afraid of the LORD that day; and he said, "How can the ark of the LORD come to me?" And David was unwilling to move the ark of the LORD into the city of David with him; but David took it aside to the house of Obed-Edom the Gittite. Thus the ark of the LORD remained in the house of Obed-Edom the Gittite three months, and the LORD blessed Obed-Edom and all his household."

At first David was unwilling to bring the Ark into Jerusalem God's way due to the death of Uzzah. **They had put it on a new cart;** and as they were dancing and praising God, as a triumphant entry coming into Jerusalem, the ark was falling, when Uzzah reached to catch it; he was struck dead. (2 Samuel 6:2-11) After this episode, David took the Ark to Obed-Edom's house because he was afraid. One thing we must remember is that David knew God's governmental order in partnering with God's apostolic plan and how he was supposed to bring the ark of God's presence on the priests' shoulders. Yet they replaced the Ark on a new cart.

Man's Way Represents the New Cart

Man's way represents the New Cart. The flesh is a mindset or a system of thinking that is in opposition to God's Word. God's Word says that flesh can't produce the things of God. The flesh can't bring forth what the Spirit wants to do supernaturally. The flesh is hostile to the ways of God; however, God's way ALWAYS brings us into liberty.

They tried to bring the presence of God in a fashion that was thought up by their own fleshly minds. Therefore, when flesh touched the ark, it brought death. Romans 8:6-8 says, "For to be carnally minded is death; but to be spiritually minded is life and peace. "Because the mind set on the flesh is hostile toward God; for it does not subject itself to the law of God, for it is not even able to do so, and those who are in the flesh cannot please God."

John 6:63 says, "It is the Spirit who gives life; the flesh profits nothing; the words that I have spoken to you are spirit and are life."

We say we want God's presence but we like to hitch His presence to some of our new carts. We like to add Him to our list of organizations, or load Him on top of the mechanics of ministry, and then off we go. I wonder how much of our service is really in the energy of the flesh. So often we put forth our hands, but not our hearts.

God is Building the House of David

God is building the HOUSE OF DAVID the way He wants it. He is taking down the old man-made mechanical structure, and HE is building a new structure of HIS GLORY bringing in the manifested PRESENCE OF GOD. And guess what? There's no competition involved. The dawning of a new day is upon us; the sons of God are arising to bring healing and transformation to our land, and we're being liberated from man-made Religion like never before!!!

The House of David represents a Corporate-House that has many members where God is granting authority to govern His kingdom on HIS EKKLESIA'S SHOULDER. The shoulder represents a place of GOD'S GOVERNMENTAL ORDER IN HIS KINGDOM.

Isaiah 22:22 says, "Then I will set the key of the house of David on his shoulder..." According to this scripture, many are being given governmental keys of authority in the house of David.

This is a pivotal time where God is setting things in HIS order so that HIS PLAN IS FULFILLED. This will be a time where God is doing away with what He did not orchestrate. When David finally realized he needed to obey God; he adjusted his heart, and obeyed God. However it came with a big price of obedience. Every six paces they sacrificed an ox and a fatling.

The Kenosis of God

David knew the power of emptying Himself in order to exalt Jesus as king. David danced right out of his kingly robe, down to a common priest's robe. He **emptied himself** of his title as the King of Israel rather than exalting his title over people in leadership, which is the same concept that Jesus did. (2 Samuel 6:14)

The Greek Word for '**emptied**' is **KENOSIS** found in Philippians 2:3-11 that says, "Do nothing from selfishness or empty conceit, but with humility of mind regard one another as more important than yourselves; do not merely look out for your own personal interests, but also for the interests of others. Have this attitude in yourselves which was also in Christ Jesus, who, **although He existed in the form of God,** did not regard equality with God a thing to be grasped, but **emptied (KENOSIS)** Himself, taking the **form of a bond-servant,** and being made in the likeness of men. Being found in appearance as a man, **He humbled Himself by becoming obedient to the point of death,** even death on a cross. **For this reason, also, God highly exalted Him,** and bestowed on Him the name which is above every name, so that at the name of Jesus EVERY KNEE WILL BOW, of those who are in heaven and on earth and under the earth, and that every tongue will confess that Jesus Christ is Lord, to the glory of God the Father."

Jesus **emptied** Himself of His deity, when He temporarily clothed Himself in the garment of a common priest while still remaining in His Deity body, as king. Jesus stepped out of HIS DIETY of glory and stepped into humanity as a Bond-servant. He understood the way up is down, which is what everyone of us will need to do, if we're going to be used by God. This is exactly what David did; God is looking for a people that will empty themselves of self-exalted places to exalt HIM as the KING.

A desire for power or control originates from religion. Genuine leaders do not dominate through power; they lead by example. Lording over someone is very demeaning, and it releases pride in leaders. (1 Peter 5:1-3) Being a bond-servant is a choice that one makes to reveal their heart to God and not to gain prominence with man. Agape love requires a great sacrifice, and a giving of oneself, like JESUS but it is a powerful gesture of sacrificial love; and when we respond in that way, it becomes as an aroma of sacrifice to God. Ephesians 5:2 says, "...Walk in love, just as Christ also loved you and gave Himself up for us, an offering and a sacrifice to God as a fragrant aroma."

2 Samuel. 6:12-23 says, "Now it was told King David, saying, "The LORD has blessed the house of Obed-Edom and all that belongs to him, on account of the ark of God." David went and brought up the ark of God from the house of Obed-Edom into the city of David with gladness. And so it was that when the bearers of the ark of the LORD had gone six paces, he sacrificed an ox and a fatling. And **David was dancing before the LORD with all his might, and David was wearing a linen ephod.** So David

and all the house of Israel were bringing up the ark of the LORD with shouting and with the sound of the trumpet."

"Then it happened as the ark of the LORD came into the city of David that **Michal the daughter of Saul** looked out of the window and **saw King David leaping and dancing before the LORD; and she despised him in her heart.** So they brought in the ark of the LORD and **set it in its place inside the tent** which David had pitched for it; and David offered burnt offerings and peace offerings before the LORD." "When David had finished offering the burnt offering and the peace offering, he blessed the people in the name of the LORD of hosts. Further, he distributed to all the people, to all the multitude of Israel, both to men and women, ...Then all the people departed each to his house."

Verse 20 says, "But when David returned to bless his household, **Michal the daughter of Saul,** came out to meet David and said, "How the king of Israel distinguished himself today! **He uncovered himself today in the eyes of his servants' maids as one**

of the foolish ones shamelessly uncovers himself!"

Many people teach that when David danced before the Lord with all his might, that he danced down to his underwear (2 Samuel. 6:12-23). This is NOT TRUE. That would be perverted.

When Michal, David's wife, looked out the window and saw David dancing in a way she never had seen before, she sarcastically rebuked him for celebrating **as a common priest, not because he danced down to his underwear** because she considered it **unbefitting for a king.** However, David did not care what man thought, including his wife, and for this she despised him for it. This action of irreverence brought a curse of barrenness on her, which separated the two of them forever.

The amazing thing is that when David brought the ark of God into Jerusalem in a way that no one had seen before, it made an immediate separation between them. Michal who represents the **old order** was Saul's offspring that **never broke away from her father's house.** She hated the new move of God;

and this means anyone who operates in the old order also hates the new move of God.

One of the greatest hindrances to the new move of God is an attachment to the old order. Many have camped around an old move of God, thinking that they have reached the peak of spirituality and enshrined the way God used to move. However that's a form of idolatry. We should desire God's freedom and experience His presence in a new way. But that is not how we're use to it; rather we often put Him in our religious boxes.

So David said to Michal, "It was before the LORD **who chose me above your father and above all his house, to appoint me ruler over the people of the LORD, over Israel; therefore, I will celebrate before the LORD.** "I will be more lightly esteemed than this and will be humble in my own eyes, but with the maids of whom you have spoken, with them I will be distinguished."

Before God transitions His people into a new place, there has to be a **separation** from the way we're use to doing church as usual. Like Michal, there will be those that will despise the "**David group**." The

"**David group**" will move into the **new order,** being led by the Spirit of God getting stronger and stronger, but the "**Saul group**" will grow weaker and weaker following the dead traditions of men. 2 Samuel 3: 1 says, "Now there was **a long war between the house of Saul and the house of David; and David grew steadily stronger, but the house of Saul grew weaker continually.**"

THEREFORE God is shifting us prophetically into His apostolic blueprint. We must not panic or be afraid of the turbulence that's arising. God is only removing those things that contradict His Word, and those things that are not compatible with HIS PLAN.

Jeremiah 15:19 says, "Therefore, thus says the LORD: "If you return, then I will restore you-- Before Me you will stand; And if you extract the precious from the worthless, you will become My spokesman." This is God separating the precious from the worthless in everyone of us; and we must allow God to purify us.

There is a divine threshing floor that is separating the precious from the vile, and it's taking place in the church right now. As already stated; Michal represents Saul's fleshly side, since she was Saul's daughter. We must be careful of what we're trying to fight, because if we're trying to fight against something that God is trying to bring forth, then we're not fighting man, but God Himself. There will be a purging away from all pride, self-exalted places that have gotten in GOD'S WAY.

The Lord wants to open the door into His secret place and if we come through that door, we will discover new revelation that will transcend our intellectual understanding, and we will be able to walk in the Spirit unhindered, as a true son of God. Galatians 5:25 says, "If we live in the Spirit, let us also walk in the Spirit."

Christian study guides and teaching manuals can be very helpful to enhance our walk with God. Yet, our greatest quest is not to follow a manual but to actually follow Emmanuel. (A name used for God in OT) This is a new day. We're going to need to follow the authentic presence and power of God if we're going to be prosperous spiritually. We cannot look to any other source, because if we're looking to being filled artificially, it will not accomplish God's purpose.

Therefore, we need to look to the Lord for His guidance and direction for our future. We are going to need God's wisdom and the ability to exercise spiritual discernment so that we can know what to do and how to handle situations that arise. Be encouraged and stay connected to the Lord because our life in the Spirit is everything, and will determine our destiny.

Chapter 3

SEASONS AND TIMES

Birthing the True Sons of God in the Earth

We're in a strategic time between that which is coming to a close and that which is just ahead. There will be a very distinct difference between where we have been and where we are going. We should watch for opportunities to extricate ourselves from hindrances that have kept us from achieving our destiny. If we can empty ourselves and let go; God will lead our steps, and we will be delighted with the new version of our life.

We are currently in a season of being upgraded, where major adjustments for many people are taking place. The Lord is positioning His people for elevation; with the heart of God to climb up on the mountaintop. The elevation is for those who are strong at heart, but humble and for those who can withstand the resistance. The elevation that God is manifesting doesn't come without a price, but the Lord has prepared us for such a time as this.

Therefore, we must remove ourselves from distractions, time stealers, and destiny destroyers. As we allow God to remove everything that's unproductive in our life, we will get divine instruction for what's ahead. God's Word encourages us to let go of the past and reach forward to the new possibilities that are ahead. Philippians 3:13 says, "Brethren, I do not count myself to have apprehended; but one thing I do, forgetting those things which are behind and reaching forward to those things which are ahead."

God promises to make our steps firm when we delight in His ways, and we will not stumble or fall because the Lord upholds us. Psalm 37:23 -24 (NASB) says, "The steps of a man are ordered by the Lord, and He delights in his way. When he falls, he will not be hurled headlong, because the Lord is the One who holds his hand."

God wants us to take the land for the glory of His kingdom. But often there are parts of our heart that have become bitter and hardened because of the difficulties we have faced. Those hard places of discouragement, rejection, and frustration must be plowed up like fallow ground and planted with seeds of faith and trust. Therefore, we must take the ground of our own heart before we can do the external work of God's kingdom.

Hosea 10:12 says, "Sow to yourselves in righteousness, reap in mercy; break up your fallow ground: for it is time to seek the LORD, till he come and rain righteousness upon you."

The Plowman will Overtake the Reaper

God is moving us away from mere tradition and into deeper revelation so that we can operate in the new things He is releasing from Heaven. We are living in the middle of prophesy spoken and prophecy being fulfilled. Amos 9:13 says, "Behold, the days are coming," says the Lord, "When the plowman shall overtake the reaper, the treader of grapes him who sows seed; the mountains shall drip with sweet wine, and all the hills shall flow with it."

In this season, many will feel like they're lagging behind but it's occurring because God's Spirit is moving us fast at a greater acceleration. What do I mean by that? I mean, as fast as we're planting, the harvest will manifest rapidly.

To many of us, it has seemed like the WORD OF THE LORD HAS BEEN DELAYED in the past but now we're moving prophetically much faster. In fact, God has been preparing our character and getting us ready to steward for what is coming. Some of it makes little sense to our natural mind, but as we wholeheartedly yield and embrace the heart of the Father, we're going to step into some WIDE EFFECTIVE DOORS that will bring great honor and glory to God's KINGDOM.

The Father is holding everything together by the power of HIS WORD. Those who desire healing in our land must come in agreement with GOD'S WORD, as we partner with God, we will see HIS POWER MANIFEST. When heaven and earth agree together, with GOD'S WORD, it brings forth deliverance, the provision, the healing, and the blessing that we've been crying out for.

Therefore we're moving into transition to move into our new season.

Transition Period

We are in a transition period, and those that yield to God in this transition are about to ascend to a higher level of spiritual existence. So it is vital to our freedom, in the letting go of what 'was', so that we can step into where we're going.

God desires His people to walk in a new glory we've never known or experienced before. And despite what we see taking place upon the earth and in the Church, it's time to wear our NEW MANTLES of AUTHORITY, so we're equipped to step into a new era of glory. It's going to bring us into an APPOINTED TIME ON GOD'S CALENDAR.

An Appointed Time

God has released an appointed time for us to put our ear to Heaven because things are changing rapidly. This is a favorable moment, and it's not just for a few, but for all who will step out and allow God's glory to shine through them.

Isaiah 60:1-5 says, "Arise shine; for your light has come, And the glory of the Lord has risen upon you. "For behold, darkness will cover the earth and deep darkness the people's; But the Lord will rise upon you, and His glory will appear upon you. "Nations will come to your light, and kings to the brightness of your rising. "Lift up your eyes roundabout and see;

They all gather together, they come to you. Your sons will come from afar, and your daughters will be carried in their arms. "Then you will see and be radiant, and your heart will thrill and rejoice; Because the abundance of the sea will be turned to you, and the wealth of the nations will come to you."

God is the ONE who orders the times and the seasons. We need to find out how to partner with God to see HIS PLANS MANIFESTED. Psalms 102: establishes God's appointed time, when He will hear and answer the prayer of the destitute so that a future generation will praise the Lord. This is a time when He will look down from Heaven and hear the groaning of the prisoner, to set free those who were doomed for death. Psalms 102:13 says, "You will arise and have compassion on Zion; (bat Tzion) for it is **time** (Eth) to be gracious to her, for **the appointed time** (Moed) has come." The first Hebrew word bolded for time is "Eth", which means 'a suitable or a fitting season, an opportunity or an appointed time'. The second Hebrew word bolded for appointed time is 'Moed', which means 'a dress rehearsal'. 'Kairos' is also another ancient Greek word used for time in God's Word around 86 times in the New

Testament, meaning "opportunity," "season," or "a time to be suited up." (e.g., in Matthew 8:29; Luke 19:44; and Acts 24:25).

The Greek word 'kairos' comes from the Greek word kara, meaning ("head") referring to things "coming to a head." Everything is "coming to a head," and it is requiring a decisive action.

The Lord Himself, when He spoke this word to me; was revealing to me we are BEING SUITED UP FOR THIS SEASON. (Praise God right there)

We need to take advantage of this moment where we have a window of favorable opportunity to obey God. God uses willing vessels to speak HIS MESSAGE. God's message is ALWAYS DELIVERED through a human instrument. Therefore, we are like a watchman on the wall–like Paul Revere's.

The Old Testament Prophets had the calling of delivering sobering messages, God told Ezekiel, "Son of man, I have made you a watchman for the house of Israel; therefore, hear a word from My mouth, and give them warning from Me." (Ezekiel 3:17) Yet God is raising a NEW BREED of WATCHMEN WHO ARE

STEPPING INTO THEIR POST CALLED 'THE WAR-ROOM OF HEAVEN' FOR THIS HOUR.

The War- Room of Heaven

We are establishing what a watchmen is for this hour. Many are being ushered into the WAR ROOM of Heaven as we're being suited up to step out for God's call to sound the alarm. God desires to raise up prophetic voices that will shake kingdoms and sound the alarm like Paul Revere did in his generation.

Yes In this hour, we will see...

—Fathers and Mothers mentoring sons and daughters to carry an apostolic mantle.

—Old prophets training new prophets who have the Elijah/Elisha anointing to accomplish double what Elijah did.

—Watchmen are being set up to prophetically see and hear what God is saying and doing in the earth to sound an alarm.

—Intercessors are being planted in specific places to reap a harvest. Intercessors are being given more strategic insights, and secret mysteries are being uncovered.

—Teachers will receive specific assignments to instruct those who have teachable hearts and will teach others.

—Father God will use Children and will astound us with what comes out of their mouths.

—Warrior women will be raised up as Paul Revere's as well. Psalm 68, prophesies about the coming of a great army of women who would experience incredible victories for the Kingdom of Christ.

Psalms 68:11-14 says, "The Lord gives the command; The women who proclaim the good tidings are a great host: "Kings of armies flee, they flee, and she who remains at home will divide the spoil!" When you lie down among the sheepfolds, you are like the wings of a dove covered with silver, and its pinions with glistening gold. When the Almighty scattered the kings there."

—Last, in this hour we will see a move of angelic activity that will ascend from earthly places to heavenly places. God is opening heaven's gate to give us angelic assistance.

Understand this Beloved, there's a battle waging, but there are many more fighting with us than those fighting against us. (2 Kings 6:16) God is sending His heavenly hosts to do battle for us, and WE ARE GOING TO WIN AND USHER IN A KINGDOM REVOLUTION.

God's Word tells us in Genesis 28 that Jacob had a dream in which he saw angels ascending and descending from Heaven to Earth. As we shift into a Kingdom Revolution, angels will be assigned to assist us as we move into our God ordained purposes.

Hebrews 1:14: says, "Are not all angels ministering spirits sent to serve those who will inherit salvation?"

A Shofar is Blown to Awaken God's People From Being Lethargic

In the Hebrew culture; On Rosh Hashanah, the Jewish people would blow the shofar to make an ANNOUNCEMENT, to awaken the people from being lethargic. Even the meaning of being prophetic means to hear a blast from Heaven. Therefore, God uses prophets like watchmen on a wall (or as I refer a lot in this Book to Paul Revere's) to sound His alarm in order to awaken something inside of His people, something that has laid dormant, so that we can be used for God's purpose.

The shofar (or ram's horn) was often used in Biblical times to break the powers of darkness over regions, atmosphere's, churches, surroundings of darkness, and households. The shofar represents God's breath blowing into the nostrils of His people, reviving them and awakening the lost and the hopeless, including believers that need encouragement.

Like Ezekiel prophesying to the dead bones of Israel, prophetic words breathe life into the dead bones of our hopelessness. Prophecy means we are speaking from the divine inspiration of God that will manifest God's purpose through our life. The word "prophecy", taken apart, is 'pro', which means before, and 'phecy', means to prepare. Therefore, prophecy is a preceding word that prepares us for our seasons to awaken something in us. God will strengthen us and will breathe life into us to bring something that has laid dormant back to life. Yes, it is so evident His purpose is being awakened in us.

Our shofar can also represent our mouth, when we release a prophetic word or we lift up our voice in proclamation through decrees and praise to God. As we praise the Lord and decree the Word of God, it will release a sound of VICTORY!!! The things that we are walking through we must aggressively push through and get HEAVEN'S DIRECTION in this season.

Therefore, let's lift our voice with decrees and prophetic proclamations over regions, atmospheres our churches, surroundings of darkness and our households and declare them to come into the KINGDOM. We can blast down the enemy's plans and they will fall null and void.

Isaiah 42: 13 says, "He will march out like a champion before you this day, like a warrior He will stir up his zeal; and with a shout he will raise the battle cry and will triumph over his enemies."

Revelations 5:5 says "Stop weeping; behold, the Lion that is from the tribe of Judah, the Root of David, has prevailed."

Job 37:2-5 says, "Listen closely to the thunder of His voice, and the rumbling that goes out from His mouth. Under the whole heaven He lets it loose, and His lightning to the ends of the earth. After it, a voice roars; He thunders with His majestic voice, and He does not restrain the lightnings when His voice is heard. God thunders with His voice wondrously, doing great things which we cannot comprehend."

Pray this as a prayer of Decree For Our Land

We the people of God declare that we have faith in God. We the people declare that once God starts something, He finishes it. We the people of God declare that our faith is strong and that we believe He is ever at work in America on our behalf. We the people declare God is drawing our young people to Himself and that through their salvation, families will be saved, healed, and delivered, and set on fire to burn with the power of God.

Father, we press in more to hear from Heaven as we see the day approaching. We are so grateful that we have a safe place beneath the Shadow of Your wing where the enemy cannot find us. His evil plans cannot touch us and Your hand covers us and keeps us, and will provide and heal us. As watchmen and gatekeepers over our nation, we declare that pestilence will NOT TOUCH YOUR PEOPLE. We the people believe that You, Jesus took upon YOURSELF every sickness and disease that hell can dream up. Hell has no creative power, so they keep releasing the same thing year after year. However in spite of what man does: we the people declare that Psalm 91 is at work on our behalf. We the people declare that the blood of Jesus, poured out at the Cross, still speaks a better Covenant today that provides everything we will ever need. We have placed that blood upon the doorposts of our home and our extended family, and the death angel cannot find us.

As watchmen on the wall of our nation(s) we declare that the atmosphere is creating an open Heaven for the Holy Spirit to breakthrough to pour out upon all flesh the promise spoken of in Joel. We simply stand in the gap for the oil from Heaven to flow down over us. Give us Your peace. How You surround us, lift us up (Psalm 3:3; Psalm 27:1-14; Psalm 34:7) and carry us. Mold us, and shape us for Your plan to come to pass. Give us greater courage, no matter what is going on around us. Give us EYES of heaven!! Yes LORD OPEN OUR SPIRITUAL EYES TO SEE IN THE SUPERNATURAL as Ephesians 1: 17-18 proclaims. Our natural eyes only tells us what is going on around us in the natural, but our spiritual eyes give us spiritual understanding. We ask You, Lord open our spiritual eyes to see what You are revealing to the TRUE SONS

OF GOD. We ask as Judah which means (PRAISE) to go up first; that the enemy's power be broken over us. We decree that his bow, his arrow, his shield, the sword and the weapons of war sent against us are being broken over us in JESUS NAME.

Psalms 44:5-7 says, "Through You we will push back our adversaries; Through Your name, we will trample down those who rise up against us. For I will not trust in my bow, nor will my sword save me. But You have saved us from our adversaries, And You have put to shame those who hate us."

Thank you, Father, that You're dismantling the enemy in every area of our life. We pray that decree for our lives, for our territory, for our families, and we pray it for the nations of the earth. By the power of YOUR authority we dismantle the weaponry of the enemy in Jesus' Name Amen!

Chapter 4

REPENTANCE, REFRESHING AND RESTORATION

Birthing the True Sons of God in the Earth

If we're going to enter a new era; we will have to think like a true son of God. There are 3 words that we're going to study in Acts 3:19-21.

They are:

Repentance

Refreshing

Restoration

Acts 3: 19-21 says, "Therefore repent and return, so that your sins may be wiped away, in order that times of refreshing may come from the presence of the Lord; and that He may send Jesus, the Christ appointed for you, whom heaven must receive until the period of restoration of all things, about which God spoke by the mouths of His holy prophets from ancient times."

The Passion Translation says, "And now you must repent and turn back to God so that your sins will be removed (obliterated or cancelled) and so that times of refreshing will stream from the Lord's presence. And He will send you Jesus, the Messiah, the Chosen One for you. For He must remain in Heaven until the restoration of all things Has taken place, fulfilling everything that God said long ago through His holy prophets."

The Word REPENTANCE

As we're studying the word 'REPENTANCE', it's good to know that the 40 days of Teshuvah alludes to the time of repentance that was linked to Moses' intercession when Israel sinned with the Golden calf (Exodus 32).

Rosh Hashanah ushers in the beginning of the Jewish year and is a holiday that celebrates the creation of the world, something that's reflected in its name, which means "head of the year" in Hebrew.

Rosh Hashanah will begin at sundown and will continue at the start of the Days of Awe, a 10-day period of reflection and repentance that concludes with Yom Kippur, on the Day of Atonement. Rosh Hashanah starts on the first days of Tishrei (the seventh month on the Hebrew calendar), which usually places it in September or October on our gorgonian calendar, and many choose to celebrate the holiday on just one day. The Theme of the Jewish High Holy Days was a holiday referred to as Teshuvah, a word often translated to 'Repentance,' but it's more accurately understood as turning back (shuv) to God.

'Teshuvah' included the 29 Days of Elul which is considered being a time of special grace and mercy when Jesus set up a BETTER COVENANT. The term 'BETTER COVENANT' means to turn back to the answer. We already know JESUS IS THE ANSWER.

In modern Hebrew; Teshuvah means an answer to a shelah or a question. God's love for us is the question, and our teshuvah—or answer is when we turn our heart toward Him. Teshuvah is one of the great gifts God gives each of us —the ability to turn back to Him and seek healing for our brokenness.

Those observing Rosh Hashanah often greet one another with the Hebrew phrase, 'shana tova' or 'L' 'Shana Tovah' meaning "Happy New Year" or "Be blessed for a good year."

According to History.com, this is a "shortened version" of the Rosh Hashanah salutation 'L'shanah tovah: May you be inscribed and sealed for a good year. Another greeting, you would say is 'teshuvah ha teshuvah' referenced to Teshuvah because both repentance and refreshing are linked to restoration in the early and the latter rain.

Focusing on the two words 'Repent' and 'Return' in Acts 3: 19 that says, "Therefore repent and return..." Both the Hebrew and Greek will add meaning to the interpretation of this scripture. The Hebrew word for 'Repent' is 'Shuv' which is the verb from teshuvah, for 'repentance' and it does not refer to being contrite (or deeply felt remorse for sins) but to change our mindset as 'a son' in our identity and to return to the Father's love in order to get our inheritance. The KJV TRANSLATION SAYS, it means to stop acting like 'a bastard.' Bastard translates to the word 'slave' or 'being illegitimate.' Yes, it literally means to return to the Father's love so that we can rule and reign with Jesus in Sonship.

Luke wrote the book of Acts. When Luke used the two Greek words 'Repent' and 'Return' in Acts 3:19 he used the Greek word 'metanoia' for 'Repent' which also means 'to change the way we think'. And then the Greek word for 'Return' is 'epistrepho' which means 'to turn back to God' or 'to be converted.'

The Word 'convert' means 'to change, to process, or mature in form, and to develop in character and function.'

There is going to be a greater freedom and liberty coming to the Body of Christ than we've ever known before when we change the way we think. We're being propelled forward and we're going to soar higher. Where our wings were once clipped in the last season; we're being restored to soar again.

God is pouring out His Spirit on His sons and daughters, and the repetitive cycles of delay and hindrance are being removed.

There are new things being established that are bringing us into a place of greater strength and new health in Christ. Things that were opposing our advancement are falling off of us, and we're going to be refreshed through repentance and turning back to God in identifying ourselves as a true son of God in our identity.

The Word REFRESHING

Next let's go to the next R in Acts 3:19-21; which is REFRESHING. TO be refreshed means 'to invigorate someone; or to stimulate them because something is new or different, or entering a change.'

The times of refreshing began at repentance when the Holy Spirit was poured out at Pentecost and it is continuing because of the culmination of Christ finished work when He died, and rose again, and ascended into the heavens to prepare for the outpouring of the 'early and the latter rain.'

One of the greatest blessings Jesus Christ left us was the ministry of the Holy Spirit. Jesus often converted many situations turning them into miracles such as He turned the water into wine, rebuked and calmed the storms, cursed fig trees, healed the lame and crippled, opened blind eyes, raised the dead, cast out devils, but everything He did; He did through the power of the Holy Spirit.

The 120 disciples met in the upper room and were filled with tongues of fire. Acts 2:1-13 says, "When the day of Pentecost had come, they were all together in one place in one accord. And suddenly a noise like a violent rushing wind came from heaven, and it filled the whole house where they were sitting. And tongues that looked like fire appeared to them, distributing themselves, and a tongue rested on each one of them. And they were all filled with the Holy Spirit and began to speak with different tongues, as the Spirit was giving them the ability to speak out."

Therefore, repentance and refreshing ushers in the early and the latter rain of refreshment from the Holy Spirit.

The Word RESTORATION

Now let's explain the last R in Acts 3:20 which is RESTORATION. The truest original text would read in Acts 3: 20 like this... "...that He may send Jesus, the Christ appointed for you. Until the restoration of all things had taken place, fulfilling everything that God has prepared for you as Sons of the MOST HIGH GOD."

The relationship between repentance, the blotting out of sins, and the times of refreshing comes from the Holy Spirt so that restoration can manifest. What is Restoration? Restoration is an act of restoring back to its original state. With this kind of restoration that

God has in mind, let's read the Lord Jesus Christ's first announcement of the Kingdom of God. Mark 1: 13-15 says, "Now after John had been been taken into custody, Jesus came into Galilee, preaching the gospel of the Kingdom saying, The time is fulfilled, and the Kingdom of God is at hand; repent and believe in the gospel." When we believe the gospel; it restores our whole being. When we think like JESUS, we know who we belong to and what our purpose is.

As already stated on the two words that Luke used in the Greek for: 'Repent' and 'Return' which mean to change the way we think. Notice the part in Acts 3: 21 that says, "... there is coming a period of restoration of all things."

What is Luke talking about? He's talking about the way we process things. Therefore, changing the way we think is the first step to restoration because it leads to perfect health. Luke's choice of the word 'Restoration' in Acts 3, is the Greek word 'Apokatastasis' which is found only here in the New Testament and is noteworthy as a medical term that means, 'restoration of perfect health.'

This is the same principle John used when he wrote, "Beloved, I pray that in all respects you may prosper be in good health, just as your soul prospers." (1 John 1:2)

The Greek Word for prosper is "Euodoo" which means 'wholeness from the inside out.' Restoration actually refers to the restoration of creation before the fall, but it refers even more so to the Davidic covenant being restored back to God's people. The Davidic Covenant is the Covenant where God promises to David and his descendants to reign on the throne and to secure the HOLY AND SURE BLESSINGS OF DAVID to His people.

The Davidic Covenant is found in 2 Samuel 7; 8-29 where God promises to David and all His descendants who will reign on the throne through Jesus Christ our Lord. And that all the HOLY and SURE blessings OF DAVID belong to us.

God secured the HOLY AND SURE BLESSINGS OF DAVID that all the descendants of David would receive a king named Messiah to take His rightful place in us. And that there is a rescue of God's people from a worldly system called Babylon.

Chapter 5

RISE UP PAUL REVERE'S...IT'S TIME FOR WAR!!!

Birthing the True Sons of God in the Earth

God is calling us to rise up like Paul Revere in this DARK HOUR AND SOUND THE ALARM to bring about a KINGDOM REVOLUTION! God isn't pacing the throne room floor wondering how He is going to get us out of this mess. He knows exactly what's going on and already has the solution to solve everything.

Jesus demonstrated His kingship with dominion and power in this earthly realm by operating in the supernatural realm, and has passed that authority to a faithful remnant who will be serving Him as TRUE SONS OF GOD, and this remnant understands the meaning of a Kingdom Revolution.

America, in a broader sense, finds herself with a vacuum of purpose. We're living in an age of crisis and spiritual tyranny, just like Paul Revere saw on the horizon in his generation. We don't have time for comfortable Christianity. The number one problem in America is a lukewarm, complacent, and silent church! There is a growing concern about the moral condition of the nation. Many people are uncertain about what's right or wrong. Many are being influenced by secularism, religious skepticism, and have been lulled to sleep through false authority, false theology, and the false prophetic. The world's system has sedated believers into deception.

God is shaking everything that is part of this man-made system so that only what He wants to remain will remain. However, it is in these predicted times our hearts must be settled and remain unshaken, since "we have received a Kingdom which cannot be shaken..." (Hebrews 12:28)

God longs for us to discern the difference between the moving of His Spirit and the moving of the enemy. Many that are sensitive to God's Spirit can pick up on the rising level of spiritual warfare in this hour in our nation. It's very clear that darkness is raging against the church. The church is experiencing everything from terror attacks, racial attacks, sexual attacks, pandemics of sickness, government tyranny, and we could name much more. God is not pleased!!

It's time that we rightly discern the signs of the times and press into God's purpose and be prepared for what's coming. We will need to be like the sons of Issachar, understanding the seasons of the time. (1 Chronicles 12:32).

Many have been saying a shift is coming, but the Lord say's it's not coming, it's ALREADY HERE!!! In the Disney Cartoon, "The Lion King," the evil brother of the King tried to get the hyenas to cooperate with his way of thinking. He told them they had to be prepared. One hyena responded by saying, "Yeah, I'm prepared! Prepared? Prepared for what?" He had no clue what he was to be prepared for.

Sad to say, but this is where most of the church is. Therefore, understanding our authority in the Kingdom of God is a must before anything can change. Authority is the power to decide, and to invoke our authority as we pray using our weapons. As a son of God, we have the supernatural ability to bind and loose. Jesus Himself declared in Matthew 16:19, "And I will give you the keys of the kingdom of heaven; and whatever you bind on earth shall have been bound in heaven, and whatever you loose on earth shall have been loosed in heaven."

As God's chosen people, we are THE ROYAL PRIESTHOOD that Christ is the king and ruler of, and we've been made HIS KINGS AND PRIESTS to stand in the GAP through prayers and intercession to stop the enemy's plans.

The Hobbit Film

God is doing something profound-superseding the ability of man, as well as giving us victory over the attacks of the enemy. The example I can compare it to, is similar to the movie called the "Hobbit" film; where there is a scene during the climactic battle, where the good warriors charge out against their wicked enemy. They went forth attacking them in a "V" formation with their king at the front. One of the characters then shouts: "Rally to the King!"

The Lord seemed to say to me when I thought about that statement; "This is the shout from Heaven and we must rally to our King!" As we rally to our King, and move behind Him with shouts of joy and victory, we will see His power and strength move in our behalf. For many of us, it has looked as though the enemy has hit the bull's-eye in the target of our life and our circumstances, but the Lord's arrow is about to split the arrow of our enemy and suddenly we will gain the victory that we so desperately need. When we partner with God; He will become the tip of the arrow that will break through every barrier that stands before us. Therefore, we must position ourselves with Him. We merely need to rally behind our KING, and His strength and power will trample down our enemies. We must be intentional to practice daily being present with our God, always being aware that He is with us, and He is continually fighting our battles.

Psalms 44:5-7 says, "Through You we will push back our adversaries; Through Your name, we will trample down those who rise up against us. For I will not trust in my bow, nor will my sword save me. But You have saved us from our adversaries, And You have put to shame those who hate us."

Micah 2:13 says, "The breaker goes up before them; they break out, pass through the gate and go out by it. So their king goes on before them, and the Lord at their head."

The Power of Intercession

Let's talk about Elijah's Kingdom revolution. Elijah was a man of prayer and intercession who brought fire down from heaven, prayed for rain during a drought, and it rained. After all the warfare with Jezebel, Elijah ran, hid in the cave and wanted to die. While in the cave, God called him out, and he received his BREAK-THROUGH.

Elijah's release came when he did something very powerful; he heard God's voice, as he wrapped his face in his mantle and got into a birthing position of intercession. The "key" to Elijah's victory that brought him out from under Jezebel's authority was "hearing" the voice of God through intercession. (1 Kings 19:11-13)

The Lord wants HIS PEOPLE to come out of the cave, position ourselves in a birthing position like Elijah did in intercession to thwart opposing forces. The Lord is calling INTERCESSORS IN THIS DESPERATE HOUR to intercede and BE HIS FEARLESS WARRIORS on the front lines of the battle because the darkness is increasing.

Let's break down some practical ways in what it means to be a warrior for Christ.

An Ox- Anointing

There is an Ox-anointing that drives a person to pray and intercede, which involves the work that nobody else wants to do. The Ox-anointing brings forth breakthrough, especially in the area where nobody knows anything about what they did, when nobody is looking, and where they won't be recognized. The Ox-anointing intercedes and cries in the evening and the dark nights of the hour while others are peacefully sleeping.

As an intercessor; they are pioneers who plow deep in the Spirit with fortitude and perseverance, paving the way into purpose for the sake of the kingdom. The Ox-anointing is a picture of great sacrifice and intercession. Intercessors are possessed with this Ox-anointing as they plow in the Spirit in prayer. They prepare a place for the Lord with deep travail, groans and utterance in the Spirit until something will manifest. (Romans 8: 26-27) Many people don't understand the mysterious gifting of intercessors, but they are precious to the Lord.

Pioneers usually gain little fame, mention, or notoriety because they're often overlooked or bypassed because their reward is from the Lord. They are tenacious for the sake of a greater harvest that they're contending for. They are often hidden and unappreciated and not recognized. They possess a fortitude of the Ox-anointing that doesn't look for the praise or the recognition of man. They get down in the dirt; in the muck and in the darkest places where their greatest fulfillment and joy is cultivated with the Lord.

Intercession is a very powerful response to the heart of God. It joins our heart to the one for whom we are praying for. We often confuse compassion with sympathy; however, sympathy is the counterfeit of compassion. Sympathy gives attention to the person in need, but it cannot deliver them. Compassion on the other hand delivers them. The Greek word for 'compassion' is 'sympatheo' which means to 'suffer with one another' or 'to be affected similarly', or 'to gush out' which links up with the word 'intercession.' Inter means 'to stand between the gap' and 'cession' means 'to stop.' God gives us the ability to feel compassion and to intercede for someone that's hurting. Therefore healing cannot occur without intercession.

Alice Smith says, "Although intercession is not listed as a gift in Ephesians 4, Romans 12, or 1 Corinthians 12, the gift of prophecy can be interchangeable with intercession." For example, the Hebrew word 'paga' which means 'to prophecy, or invade by violence, or to contend with an adversary, to fight or labor in fervent prayer, with force, to press forward, or seize, to catch, to travail, and weep, or to come between.' The Hebrew word 'massa' is also translated 'to prophecy a burden' or 'to declare an utterance.'

Where are those who are anointed with the ox-nature of Christ? Psalm 92:10 says, "But You have exalted my horn like that of of the wild ox; I have been anointed with fresh oil..." Therefore we see; the anointing oil will freely flow upon those who are called to minister in the Ox-anointing.

Intercessors are like PIONEERS who prepare the way with intercession, laying their lives down, with incredible suffering, pain and turmoil. They are pioneers in the Spirit. We can express intercession through prayer in a variety of ways. Those called to the office of intercession carry a heavy spiritual weight in the Spirit before the throne of God. Matthew 22: 14 says, "Many are called but few are chosen". God chooses those who respond appropriately, prepare diligently, sacrifice willingly, and know how to partner with God.

There is a significant shift coming as we yield to the Ox-anointing and it will shift many into deliverance in this next generation. The chains that have held this generation tightly are going to be set free. This generation desperately needs this anointing more than ever. In order for us to receive the harvest of souls, we need those who will pioneer the Ox-anointing in intercession to bring the KINGDOM REVOLUTION MANDATE on the scene.

The Ministry of John; the Baptist

John the Baptist pioneered the way as he introduced Jesus when he baptized Him in the Jordan River. The scripture says, ... "Jesus came from Nazareth in Galilee and was baptized by John in the Jordan. John appeared in the wilderness preaching a baptism of repentance for the forgiveness of sins. And all the country of Judea was going out to him, and all the people of Jerusalem; and they were being baptized by him in the Jordan River, confessing their sins."

John was clothed with camel hair and wore a leather belt around his waist, and his diet was locusts and wild honey. And he was preaching, saying, "After me One is coming who is mightier than I, and I am not fit to bend down and untie the straps of His sandals. I baptized you with the water of repentance; but He will baptize you with the Holy Spirit." And immediately coming up out of the water, He saw the heavens opening, and the Spirit, like a dove, descending upon Him; and a voice came from the heavens saying. "You are My Beloved Son; in You I am well pleased."

John prepared the way for the coming of Jesus, the Messiah, as a forerunner. Mark 1:2-9 says, "... just as it is written in Isaiah the prophet: "Behold, I am sending My messenger before You, who will prepare the way; The voice of one calling out in the wilderness, 'Prepare the way of the Lord, Make His paths straight!'"

Yes, for sure, John the Baptist was a pioneer who paved the way for Jesus to manifest His glory. Pioneers, like John, are forerunners who are all about establishing new roads and a willingness to plow deep into new revelation with prayers and intercession.

Pioneering New Ground

Some of you have pioneered hard places and in doing so; you became a catalyst who has sparked a flame in people's lives whether they know it or not. That flame has simultaneously sparked a Kingdom Revolution, but it also sparks criticism. A genuine move of God always causes offense to those stuck in past ways. It's important to understand there will always be those from past seasons who are unwilling to move into the new, who choose to criticize because they were unwilling to accept the new that has come.

Perhaps it was your own family who turned their backs on you, and those you once regarded as friends have walked away. But in this KINGDOM REVOLUTION, God is training you; and if your ability to trust is gone, just remember this; it isn't about trust in others, it's about trust in the ONE who called and sent you.

Don't look back to those who have withheld affirmation or denied you any recognition—Our Father affirms you THIS DAY. Remember that He is the ONE who says to you, "Well done, My good and faithful servant." God sees how you've fiercely protected that which He entrusted you with. It doesn't matter if at times you didn't even do it exactly right. He sees and knows your heart—and He loves you. Therefore, don't seek someone's approval of your gift. Seek God's approval over your life. As His light shines through you, He will make a way and a place for you.

Prophets, pioneers and intercessors are often considered strange or different because they are different. They move to the beat of a different drummer. They don't go down paved roads, instead they make roads. They move ahead to take ground, seeing what they did not yet see, calling it out and into existence through prayer. To the world, sometimes even to the Church, they are often strange and unaccepted. Some prophets are called to walk out and demonstrate what God has spoken; yet have walked through some very difficult and persecuted places.

Allow me to encourage you. If you're one of those who plow in the Spirit as a PIONEER, most likely people have misjudged you and misinterpreted your actions. You have asked God why they don't see your heart, as people have written you off, turned their backs or attacked you when your intent was simply to help. And you've asked God over and over again, "Why does this happen?"

An Isolated Season

There may be one season or several where God will isolate you to do HIS FINAL WORK WITHIN YOUR HEART. Think about John, Jeremiah, Elijah, Elisha, or even Joseph. These were just weird at times; but they had a powerful call of God on their life. I can't emphasize enough how crucial time alone with the Lord is as we go deeper into the heart of God. Remember, every ending has a new beginning. For every great season, prior to it; there will come a time in our experience we will have to sit alone. There will be times we cannot go with the crowd, we cannot enjoy the things the crowd enjoys, we cannot laugh at the foolish jokes that others laugh at, we cannot enjoy their pleasure because God is doing something sacred inside of us.

Personally, God stops me sometimes of being with the crowd, (not always but sometimes) and He will say, "I don't want you to go to that." There may not be anything wrong with what is happening there, but God just doesn't want me there. Therefore, I could not go to the places they went to, I could not read the things they read, I couldn't listen to the things they listened to, I couldn't talk the way they talked; I was isolated. Why? Because God had laid His hand on me. This is what it means to lean into OUR BELOVED and listen to HIS STILL SMALL VOICE.

This is a message, especially to those whose identities have been denied. This is your day of identity, to recognize who you are and who He created you to be. Quit trying to be someone else. Quit trying to fit in, because with some, you never will. You are simply called to be who He has called you to be and do what He has called you to do. And nothing more.

Not all pioneers will be a John; you may be more like Jeremiah or Joseph. But certainly not a single prophet or pioneer has ever had a smooth road, because remember, they make the road.

Spiritual Gates & Watchman DEFINED

Let's break this down as we're understanding what the role of a watchmen at the gate is and what it meant to guard in prayer and intercession to bring the purposes of God in the earth.

How does God use the role of watchmen to warn and teach today? What does it mean as a New Testament Watchmen to sound an alarm to this dark world to this next generation? The body of Christ needs Paul Revere's who can rightly discern the moving of the Lord—and the moving of the enemy. Isaiah 62: 6 says, "On your walls, O Jerusalem, I have appointed watchmen; All day and all night they will never keep silent."

The word watchmen represents intercession. In the Hebrew, Strong's Concordance H6822 root word: WATCHMEN means: - (1) destined, (2), keep watch (3), lookout (4), to watch expectantly (5) or to spy on.

In the Old Testament there were gates that were used to enter and exit the city. The gates had to be strong and large. Each gate had a specific purpose, and they assembled often at the gates where the elders of a city made major decisions. Peter warned us to, "Be sober and watchful, because your adversary the devil walks around as a roaring lion, seeking whom he may devour. Resist him firmly in the faith" (1 Pet. 5:8-9). The amplified translation of verse 9 says to "withstand him; be firm in faith [against his onset—rooted, established, strong, immovable, and determined]." You can't withstand something you aren't willing to confront. It is dangerous not to sound the alarm about the enemy's plots and plans. You cannot conquer an enemy that you're in agreement with or that you don't know exists.

Paul clearly warned us not to be ignorant of the devil's devices (2 Corinthians 2:11). James instructs us to "submit ourselves to God, resist the devil and he will flee" (James 4:7). We can't resist a devil if we don't discern danger and declaring what we see as a watchmen—or even if we should ignore it.

Watch Towers

Every believer has been given a different spiritual gate of authority to guard and to take it back for God. All the way back to Abraham, a prophetic promise in Genesis 22 speaks about SPIRITUAL GATES OF AUTHORITY saying, and "your seed shall possess the GATE of their enemies." (Genesis 22:17)

"WHERE ARE YOU WATCHMEN?" Yes, can you hear Him calling you?

The Lord says, "I AM sending you forth as a forerunner releasing you into new places with new assignments, meeting new relationships, and even taking you into new levels of intimacy with ME!"

The Father would encourage you to BE ANXIOUS FOR NOTHING, and to fret not, but RECEIVE HIS REST for the secrets of the Father's heart are being revealed to you. He is releasing you into a new place that seems unfamiliar, and you will not only come alive in greater ways to what He's called you to do but you will be refreshed for what this season will bring into your life.

The Lord will break the confines that have held you back and He will move you into a deeper place of carrying His heart to the people. Therefore do not take thought about tomorrow nor take this invitation lightly, for you are being invited into a place of receiving the greatest treasure of all, which is HIS HEART.

This is a heart transformation not only into His heart, but a heart transformation for the people, for the places that He's calling you to. The Lord would have you to know that this call doesn't come without great cost. The Father is looking for those who will steward His heart with integrity, purity, and not use His heart for personal gain or impure motives.

The Father is looking for His TRUE SONS OF GOD THAT WILL SURRENDER AND BE YIELDED TO HIS DIVINE PARTNERSHIP WITH HIM. AS He is inviting you into A TRUE HEART TRANSFORMATION, you will cry out TO HIM SAYING , "Lord, help me to steward YOUR heart well TO THE PEOPLE!!"

God is raising a NEW BREED of WATCHMEN WHO ARE STEPPING INTO THEIR POST PREPARING THE WAY FOR THE COMING OF THE LORD. Wow! Think about that!

In the ancient biblical days, they placed large watchtowers overlooking the fields. Throughout the weeks, as the crops were ripening toward harvest, men would stand watch, guarding the fields from animals or from thieves who would try to take off with the crops. They positioned the watchmen in a spot where they could monitor and warn others of approaches of an enemy to the town. If a threat appeared, he would sound a warning and the town would shut its gates and prepare for battle. It's not like us if we're low on food, we just go to the grocery store and get what we need. With the community's basic food stores at stake, the watchmen's role was critical to the townspeople.

Like the prophet Habakkuk; who was a watchmen, stood guard at his post. Habakkuk 2:1-3 says, "I will stand on my guard post and station myself on the rampart; and I will keep watch to see what He will speak to me, and how I may reply when I am reproved. Then the LORD answered me and said, "Record the vision and inscribe it on tablets that the one who reads it may run. For the vision is yet for the appointed time; It hastens toward the goal, and it will not fail. Though it tarries, wait for it; for it will certainly come, it will not delay."

Therefore, as king's rule and priests invoke the plan of God through prayers of intercession, this reveals we have a kingdom mandate. Even though it seems like the attacks against us have been relentless, we must not give ourselves over to discouragement and despair. We must stand strong regardless of the forces that are opposing God's plan and pray in agreement to stop the enemy's plans.

We are called to take dominion. Dominion is the power to act through legal authority. Our calling as kings and priests unto God means He's given us authority to rule, to invade, to occupy, to govern, and to administrate.

The following are some definitions to understand our purpose as Kings and Priests who are commissioned by God.

- To rule means to exercise authority.
- To possess means to invade, occupy, and take over.
- To administrate means to manage affairs.

Therefore, God is restoring what Adam lost in the garden. God created Adam as a king that would manage a kingdom even in the garden. To understand our authority, we need to understand the first great commission of dominion. Genesis 1: 26 says, "Then God said, "Let us make mankind in Our image, according to our likeness; and Let them rule over the fish of the sea and over the birds of the sky and over the livestock and over all the earth, and over every crawling thing that crawls on the earth."

Kingship is a powerful mandate that God is restoring in the earth. This mandate shows us as kings of a royal priesthood in Christ, who are governing His kingdom. 1 Peter 2:9 says, "But you are a chosen generation, a royal priesthood, a holy nation, a peculiar people; that you should show forth the praises of Him who has called you out of darkness into His marvelous light."

Kingship is an important message because how we see ourself determines how we approach the throne of God. Hebrews 4:16 says, "Therefore let's approach the throne of grace with confidence, (or boldly) so that we may receive mercy and find grace for help at the time of our need."

We are seated in Christ in heavenly places who have been given spiritual authority to govern and to rule and reign with Jesus. Ephesians 2:4-6 says, "But God, being rich in mercy, because of His great love with which He loved us, even when we were dead in our wrongdoings, made us alive together with Christ (by grace you have been saved), and raised us up with

Him, and seated us with Him in the heavenly places in Christ Jesus..."

The next chapter will reveal some practical steps that we're being trained for to contend for the victory through a process. Similar to a spiritual boot camp. Therefore, get ready people of God, the Lion from the TRIBE OF JUDAH HAS PREVAILED, and He will march out like a CHAMPION like a WARRIOR WITH A SHOUT; HE WILL RAISE THE BATTLE CRY THROUGH HIS PEOPLE AND WE WILL TRIUMPH OVER HIS AND (OUR) ENEMIES.

This is God's plan; and not man's. We will prevail because the Lion from the TRIBE OF JUDAH finished the VICTORY. We've read the end of God's final Word, and it is a FIXED FIGHT.

Part 2

THE KINGDOM REVOLUTION
PROCESS

Birthing the True Sons of God in the Earth

God is leading His Paul Revere's into a NEW PROPHETIC MOVE. I have included in the following pages as a guide that breaks down some prophetic steps; however, these steps aren't a formula and it is not an all-inclusive list. We must always be led by the Spirit. (Romans. 8:14)

In this NEW PROPHETIC MOVE, the following needs to be considered. God is going to give us a new separation, a new skin, new spiritual sight, a new speech, a new sound, a new song, and new spiritual warfare strategies that will move us into a new season.

New Separation
In the new prophetic move, we will be separated from everyone that's not going with us in our new season.

Your NEW season POSSIBLY will require a NEW SEPARATION from the people you're with right now.

We can't receive what God has for us until we release what He is trying to take away. Our progress cannot occur without leaving something or someone behind. We cannot fully enter our new season without giving up our right to the old season. If we're still tied to the old season, it will be impossible for us to enter our new season. This is very important in the SHIFT. In fact, you'll find out really fast who you need to be with and who you need to separate from. There will be those who will honor what God has put within you; and there will be those that will dishonor what God has put within you.

SOMETHING TO THINK ABOUT; WITHOUT honor there is NO IMPARTATION.

Wheat, Tare, & Chaff Study

I recently did a study on wheat, tares and chaff. The wheat represents 'the sons of the Kingdom' and what God's Word calls 'tares' is commonly known today as 'weeds or the false wheat' called 'the wicked' (or Religious People). The tares are people that say; they are sons of God's Kingdom but aren't acting like it, because religion has hardened their heart.

Just to reemphasize: Jesus tells us in Matthew 13 what these things represent. He said the field is the world; the wheat (good seed) are the sons of the kingdom of God; and the tares (bad seed) are the sons of the kingdom of the world.

The disciples came to Jesus and said, "Explain to us the parable of the weeds of the field." After He explained it to them, He said **the weeds are the sons of the evil one** and **the enemy who sowed them is the devil**. Then He said to them, 'An enemy has done this.' The servants said to Him, 'Do you want us to go and gather them up?' But He said, 'No lest while you gather up **the tares** you also uproot **the wheat** with them. Let both grow together until the harvest and at the time of harvest I will say to the reapers, first gather together the tares and bind them in bundles to burn them but gather the wheat into my barn." (Matthew 13:28-30)

According to Matthew 13, it is hard to distinguish between the wheat and tare in the early stages, so as they grow together until the difference between the two becomes apparent. Then the good wheat is threshed or sifted through another process, to separate the **chaff**. Now, the **chaff** represents the things that **God is separating from us as sons of the kingdom to mature and purify us**.

Often in Biblical days, a threshing floor was a process used to separate the good wheat from the chaff. Chaff is referred to as useless. As they threshed the grain, they used a wooden shovel for tossing the grain up against the wind. In this process, the lighter chaff would blow away in the wind, leaving the good wheat to settle in a pile.

There are times God will allow Satan to sift some things in our life to reveal something that's in us that He wants to remove, but not to destroy us. Remember, in Luke 22:31-32 the Lord said to Peter, "Simon, Simon, behold, Satan hath desired to have you, that he may **sift** you as wheat: But I have prayed for thee, that thy faith fails not: and when thou art converted, strengthen thy brethren."

Another translation says, "Simon, Simon, behold, Satan has demanded permission to sift you like wheat; but I have prayed for you, that your faith may not fail; and you, when once you have turned again, strengthen your brothers."

Jesus is the ONE WHO WINNOWS THE WHEAT, and not Satan. When the wheat is ready for harvest, there are tiny black seeds in the grain's head, and when this shows up; the wheat is heavy and must be harvested quickly before the bad ruins the good.

Matthew 3:12 says, "His winnowing fork is in His hand, and He will thoroughly clear His threshing floor; and He will gather His wheat into the barn, but He will burn up the chaff with unquenchable fire."

When God wants to separate something from our life, He throws the bad things away and pulls out the good He wants us to keep. Yes, God is threshing and separating all the bondages in our life; the works of the flesh, all baggage like offense, grudges, religion, condemnation, even our own self-judgments, unforgiveness, and the breaking of ungodly soul ties. Presently, two things are going on in the spirit realm; a separation from the chaff in our life and people who are not going where we are going.

The wheat that bows over low is symbolic of humility before the Lord as a symbol of surrender and yet when observing the tare; it stands straight up. This is significant revealing that the one that stands straight up represents tares who are people that are being proud and self-exalting, and promoting themselves. But the wheat that was heavy bows over low which reveals humility. Therefore, this is why God uses a threshing process in our life to separate the wheat from the tares.

The Surrendered Ones

Those who are walking in pride and arrogance have not walked in the low places with the Lord. They are certainly not surrendered. Those who have not yielded to God's process of surrender and being refined in the refiner's fire will be demoted. They will not stand in God's special season He has ordained for their lives. However, those who will surrender to God's refining process will be promoted.

The surrendered ones are a remnant being called out to impact the world for God's Kingdom. They've endured many trials, storms, and tragedies that would've knocked most people out of the saddle, but they have continued to press through no matter what. The surrendered ones will be the CARRIERS OF GOD'S GLORY. They are not looking to control or manipulate what God is doing, because they are

LOVERS OF HIS GLORY. Therefore, we're being prepared as the BRIDE of Christ through stages of surrender as we are preparing for God's prophetic purposes. In this surrendering process, there will be a distinction between the called and the chosen. Many are called, but few are willing to pay the price to be chosen. "So, the last shall be first, and the first last: for many be called, but few chosen." (Matthew 20:16)

The Eye of the Needle

Have you heard of the 'Eye of the Needle'? In the Middle Eastern culture, there was a gate called the Eye of the Needle. The gate was so small it required them to dismount the animal they were riding (their transportation in that culture), to unload all their possessions and bow down low to get through the gate. This gate is a picture of complete surrender to God and letting Him have first place in our life. (Luke 18:24-25)

The Lord is bringing His people through a surrender process, but once we yield to Him, the sooner we do, the sooner we can move forward. We often try to hold on and grieve over our losses, but if we will just learn to let go and let God take us where He wants to take us; then the process can begin. We say we want the place of blessing, but we don't want to go through the process of surrender. As God takes us through the narrow place, we will feel the pressure, but that is how God prepares us to let go; so we can be commissioned into a NEW PLACE.

Divine Arrangements

As I was meditating one day on all this separation that Jesus is doing specifically in the church, both corporately and individually; God brought the cave of Adullam to my mind. God called David to the cave of Adullam along with 400 of His Mighty men to train them for what was ahead. 1 Samuel 22: 2-3 says, "So, David departed from there and escaped to the cave of Adullam; and when his brothers and all his father's household heard of it, they went down there to him. Everyone who was in distress, and everyone who was in debt, and everyone who was discontented gathered to him; and he became a captain over them. Now there were about four hundred men with him. And David went from there to Mizpah of Moab; and he said to the king of Moab, "Please let my father and my mother come and stay with you until I know what God will do for me".

The Cave of Adullam is a Picture of the Church being Transitioned

The Cave of Adullam is a picture of the Church being transitioned from one place into another, to prepare us for God's higher prophetic purpose, and I believe this is exactly where the church is RIGHT NOW.

God used the Cave of Adullam to PREPARE DAVID, and a company of people who were a remnant to prepare them for God's higher purpose. Adullam (uh duhl' luhm) means "a sealed off place, or to turn aside in the sense of - to hide or seek refuge or retreat."

God drew 400 men who were in DISTRESS, DEBT, and DISCONTENTED to join David for a great VICTORY.

Everyone who was IN DISTRESS -

Everyone who was IN DEBT-

Everyone who was DISCONTENTED -

The word 'distress,' means someone who is oppressed by an enemy.'

The word 'debt,' means 'the state of owing.'

The word 'discontented,' means 'a lack of peace of mind, or to be dissatisfied.'

The people that came to David weren't satisfied serving under a king who was not hearing from God and was leading the nation in disobedience against the direction of the Lord. So, they came to David to receive direction, protection, and training. HOWEVER, before God transitioned David into his place of KINGSHIP, David served and waited on Saul in the palace, who was Israel's leader. After this time of serving, David was then separated from Saul in the palace and brought into the cave of Adullam to wait for God's next instruction. David was in a time of transition between that which was ending and that which was just ahead.

A Higher Level

When God is getting ready to promote us to a higher level, we will recognize the dismantling of one season, so that we can move with God's new commission. If we want victory in our life, we've got to submit our lives to the Lord and surround ourselves with the people He puts us with. We must let God make us into one of His WARRIORS.

The Cave of Adullam

In the passage of 1 Samuel 22:2-3 each man had to make a choice: they could keep on staying with Saul who operated in disobedience or they could take their stand in the Cave of Adullam with David, God's new chosen king.

David had to learn to wait on God in the darkness of this cave, because that is where he prepared his heart before God. He stayed fixed on what the higher purpose was. David's own words were, "My heart is fixed, O God, my heart is fixed: I will sing and give praise." (Psalm 57:7)

When I think of something that is fixed, I think about the pendulum on a clock. How does the pendulum on a clock stay so consistent and swing the same way back and forth? It's because the pendulum is centered and fixed and that's exactly what God is requiring of us, that we are centered and fixed on HIM.

Isaiah 26: 3 says, "The steadfast of mind You will keep in perfect peace, because he trusts in You."

New Skin

In the new prophetic move, you will be made into a New Wineskin

To get into your new season, you'll have to live in a NEW WINESKIN. This means something must break in our life before we are made new. God wants to teach us new things, but He will break something in our life; before He can renew us. Most of the church is still living within an old wineskin or under an old paradigm that is out of season. We want the power of God in a fresh new way, but we can't hold it or handle it until we are given a NEW WINESKIN.

God will not give us 'THE NEW', in an old wineskin, because we will waste it. We're looking for the NEW, but our structure can't hold it.

The new glory will not fit in the old wineskin because it will blow many churches up by causing division. Therefore if we aren't separated from the old structure (religious tradition) and made flexible to hold the new wine, we will burst, and it will ruin. Matthew 9:17 says, "Nor do people put new wine into old wineskins; otherwise the wineskins burst, and the wine pours out and the wineskins are ruined; but they put new wine into fresh wineskins, and both are preserved."

Religious Tradition

Religious tradition hinders the new wine; they've been so conditioned to stay in the old wineskins, because they don't know how to move forward. People like this remind me of how circus elephants are trained. Trainers who trained circus elephants would tie young elephants to large stakes with heavy chains that kept them confined for a while. When this method is done consistently, young elephants realize their movement is limited and they cannot break the chains, so they remain confined. When the elephant becomes an adult, the heavy chains are replaced with a flimsy rope that could easily be broken. What's happening? Why can't the adult elephant break free from the flimsy rope? It's because they conditioned the elephant to a learned pattern of limitation. (WOW)

We've been so conditioned by religion that we're still acting like we're still bound up to the traditions of men, and we're still thinking through an old church mindset. God is trying to transition us into experiencing His presence in a fresh way, but we still have an old mindset.

The Process of Making a New Wineskin

The process of making a new wineskin is they would scrape out the essence of the old wine, and then soak the wineskin in fresh oil so there will be some elasticity and some flexibility. When God wants to do something new in us, He will stretch us and pull us into places we are unfamiliar with.

When Jesus performed His first miracle at the Wedding of Cana, He saved the best wine for last. God is saving the BEST WINE reserved for the end of the Church Age. We are the new wineskins that God wants to pour HIS GLORY through, but if we're still living on the OLD WINE (REVELATION), we can't hold the NEW WINE.

Therefore, we'll have to understand how to break old mindsets in order to build new mindsets.

Prophetic People are Iconoclastic

Prophetically speaking, to receive the new wine, we're going to have to be both iconoclastic (TO BREAK) and innovative (TO BUILD).

Prophetic people are both iconoclastic and innovative. An iconoclastic person is someone who engages in 'being iconoclastic' which is 'the breaking of something before the building of it.'

The power of the prophetic comes in to destroy old beliefs, religious mindsets, and hardened hearts that need to be demolished for there to be an opening for the love of the Father to come in. Therefore, it first uproots and destroys those strongholds before it can build, plant or construct something new.

Jeremiah 1:5-10 says, "Before I formed you in the womb I knew you, and before you were born I consecrated you; I have appointed you a prophet to the nations." Then I said, "Alas, Lord GOD! Behold, I do not know how to speak, because I am a youth." But the LORD said to me, "Do not say, 'I am a youth,' because everywhere I send you, you shall go, and all that I command you, you shall speak. "Do not be afraid of them, for I am with you to deliver you," declares the LORD. Then the LORD stretched out His hand and touched my mouth, and the LORD said to me, "Behold, I have put My words in your mouth. "See, I have appointed you this day over the nations and over the kingdoms, To pluck up and to break down, To destroy and to overthrow, To build and to plant."

Watchman Nee

Watchman Nee said, 'the prophetic needs to create 'a beachhead' in the Spirit. What does the term 'beachhead' mean? A 'beachhead' is a military term. When an army wants to invade and take ground, it sends its toughest fighting troops ahead of the army to land on a spot to take a small foothold of ground.

D-Day

This happened on D-Day (also known as The Normandy Landings) in 1944, when the Allied forces retook ground from the Nazis and went forward to win the war. Someone graphically portrayed the taking of the beachhead on Omaha Beach in the opening scene of the film, "Saving Private Ryan."

Once the beachhead was taken; then the regular army could go in and land, bringing in more troops and supplies and eventually expand the territory into a bigger area, to take more ground. So this is why in the spiritual realm, God will often use a forerunner to create a beachhead. God knows how pertinent it is to destroy old mindsets, so that now something new can be built.

Prophetic People are Innovative

Prophetic people are not ONLY iconoclastic but they are also innovative, therefore this comes out of a fresh revelation from GOD. In saying this, we must allow nothing to get away from the Scriptures because if it is not balanced or doesn't declare the 'whole counsel of God,' then we don't embrace it.

Not New Theology

Although it is not really creating new theology, the new revelation that God is revealing seems like new theology to those who receive it, but it's just not been revealed to us before.

Therefore, hearing with the prophetic ear has a focused punch, and it may get very messy,—but it is enough to open the heart of the people to transform them from the inside out, so that God can do something brand new to open their spiritual eyesight for the new things He desires to accomplish in their life.

New Spiritual Sight born out of Intimacy

To get into your NEW Season, you'll have to have a NEW SPIRITUAL SIGHT

There will be NEW SPIRITUAL SIGHT given in this next prophetic move, but it will come through a deeper intimacy.

Isaiah 43:18-19 says, "Do not call to mind the former things, or ponder things of the past. Behold, I will do something new, now it will spring forth; will you not be aware of it? I will even make a roadway in the wilderness, rivers in the desert."

Give us Doves Eyes

There is a beautiful scripture in Song of Solomon where the dove is found in the cleft of the Rock. Solomon says to his Bride, which typified what Jesus says to His Church who is His Bride, "O my dove, in the clefts of the rock, In the secret place of the steep pathway, Let me see your form, Let me hear your voice; For your voice is sweet, And your form is lovely." (Song of Solomon 2:14)

The dove is a symbol of endearment, submission and grace. The dove also is a symbol of the Holy Spirit. Yet here the Bridegroom calls His Bride, 'HIS DOVE', which is a very affectionate term that represents gentleness and grace as she hides herself in the cleft of the Rock with JESUS, HER BELOVED. And He says, "Let me see your form and let me hear your voice." Oh, how Jesus longs for us to spend quality time with Him, and He wants to hear our voice and listen to what He wants to say to us, AS HIS BRIDE.

If you do a study of doves, it shows that the DOVE IS THE ONLY BIRD, that has one mate in her lifetime. As she hides herself in the cleft of the rock, in the secret place of the steep pathway, (One version says in the secret place of the stairs; which means greater revelation), she is filled with single devotion toward her BELOVED. A dove has a very unusual quality because it has no side vision (meaning no peripheral vision). This means as we hide in Jesus, He opens our eyes to have undistracted devotion to Him. Oh may we grasp this people of God. Our secret life is the central key to an overcoming life, as we tap into the unconditional love of God that can heal any wound in our soul. Sermons and teachings are edifying, but they can never replace the power that we find as we sit at His feet and hear His voice in an intimate setting in the secret place.

Therefore, my prayer is: Lord, give me undistracted devotion for YOU like that. That's really all that matters. Help me push away everything that distracts me from YOU and look into YOUR eyes. Unlock the treasure within; and capture my heart, Lord, for only YOU.

Psalm 45 is A Coronation Song Sung To His Bride

One day, I was meditating on Psalms 45 and the Lord gave me some powerful revelation about His love for His Bride. Psalm 45 is a song of love or a marriage-song between Christ and His church, HIS BEAUTIFUL BRIDE. This Psalm is SO POWERFUL AS WE UNDERSTAND WHO WE ARE AND WHO WE BELONG TO IN A VERY WICKED WORLD.

AS I STUDIED THIS, it describes the beauty of the royal BRIDE IN HOW SHE HEARS THE BRIDEGROOM'S proposal to her, saying she had an eternal throne that was promised to the house of David in a marriage covenant.

This is a coronation song sung by JESUS TO HIS BRIDE, the church. As the guest arrives to the wedding, they will assemble in the wedding chamber.

Notice in Psalms 45; AS SHE IS intimate with her KING IN WORSHIP, she transforms into A WARRING BRIDE. As we worship, our king dresses us for the battles that are ahead. In Psalm 45: 1-7 says, "My heart overflows with a good theme; I address my verses to the King; My tongue is the pen of a ready writer. You are fairer than the sons of men; Grace is poured upon Your lips; Therefore, God has blessed You forever. Gird Your sword on Your thigh, O Mighty One, In Your splendor and Your majesty! And in Your majesty ride on victoriously, For the cause of truth and meekness and righteousness; Let your right hand teach you awesome things. Your arrows are sharp; The peoples fall under You; Your arrows are in the heart of the King's enemies. Your throne, O God, is forever and ever; A scepter of uprightness is the scepter of Your kingdom. You have loved righteousness and hated wickedness; Therefore God, Your God, has anointed You With the oil of joy above Your fellows."

Some theologians even say Psalms 45 is a pronounced benediction song called "Shoshanim" that means "LILIES." It is definitely a wedding proposal from our KING to HIS BELOVED BRIDE.

THERE IS A POWERFUL description of the magnificent fragrances that are released from her bosom as she worships Her Beloved. Verse 8 says, "All your garments are fragrant with Myrrh, and Aloes and Cassia; Out of ivory palaces, stringed instruments have made you glad. Kings' daughters are among Your noble ladies; At Your right hand stands the queen in gold from Ophir. Listen, O daughter, give attention and incline your ear: Forget your people and your father's house; Then the King will desire your beauty. Because He is your Lord, bow down to Him. The daughter of Tyre will come with a gift; The rich among the people will seek your favor. The King's daughter is all glorious within; Her clothing is interwoven with gold. She will be led to the King in embroidered work; The virgins, her companions who follow her, Will be brought to You. They will be led forth with gladness and rejoicing; they will enter into the King's palace."

Living from the Inside Voice

As we allow those intimate encounters with our King; worship can bubble up spontaneous songs up out of our spirit within us. Ephesians 6:10 in the Passion

Translation says, "Be supernaturally infused with strength through your life-union with the Lord Jesus. Stand victorious with the force of His explosive power flowing in and through you."

Something that I believe God is fashioning within the heart of His Bride is a deeper level of confidence that originates out of intimacy. Intimacy will awaken her with the fire and passion for her Bridegroom. He is longing for us to know Him intimately, and to put our ear next to His chest, knowing we are HIS BELOVED and He will reveal fresh revelation to us.

We were designed for intimacy and to hear His voice through our spirit man. You can talk all day to the head, filling it with knowledge, but the shift will come in our life when we live from the inside voice through intimacy with the Lord. The way we will defeat the enemy is when we realize we have the GREATER ONE living inside of us who is the God of our DESTINY! This even is confirmed through the testimony of the Apostle Paul.

Paul's Testimony

In Acts 22, Paul is downloading his life testimony, and how God revealed His ministry to Him personally. It's something we can all glean from. Acts 22:3-15 says, "I am a Jew, born in Tarsus of Cilicia, but brought up in this city, educated under Gamaliel, strictly according to the law of our fathers, being zealous for God just as you all are today. "I persecuted this Way to the death, binding and putting both men and women into prisons, as also the high priest and all the Council of the elders can testify. From them I also received letters to the brethren and started off for Damascus in order to bring even those who were there to Jerusalem as prisoners to be punished. "But it happened that as I was on my way, approaching Damascus about noontime, a very bright light suddenly flashed from heaven all around me, and I fell to the ground and heard a voice saying to me, 'Saul, Saul, why are you persecuting Me?' And I answered, 'Who are You, Lord?' And He said to me, 'I am Jesus the Nazarene, whom you are persecuting.' "And those who were with me saw the light, to be sure, but did not understand the voice of the One who was speaking to me. And I said, 'What shall I do, Lord?' And the Lord said to me, 'Get up and go on into Damascus, and there you will be told of all that has been appointed for you to do.' But since I could not see because of the brightness of that light, I was led by the hand by those who were with me and came into Damascus. A certain Ananias, a man who was devout by the standard of the Law, and well-spoken of by all the Jews who lived there, came to me, and standing near said to me, 'Brother Saul, receive your sight!' And at that very time I looked up at him. "And he said, 'The God of our fathers has appointed you to know His will and to see the Righteous One and to hear an utterance from His mouth. 'For you will be a witness for Him to all men of what you have seen and heard."

Never forget that God will lead us like Paul, but we must shift from living from the outside voices of the world to living from the inside voice. Proverbs 8:34 (NIV) says, "Blessed are those who listen to me, watching daily at my doors, waiting at my doorway."

Until we learn to live listening to the inside voice of our Beloved; we will not hear from God to walk out His plan in our lives. There has been so much dysfunction to the sheep's identity in the body of Christ alone. It's sad, but what's happened is many in the Body of Christ have exchanged busyness with

Kingdom purpose and now they're wondering why they feel so dead inside.

If we're so busy doing so many things, but we haven't found the ONE THING that God's called us to, it means we've set our focus on the wrong thing. David said in Psalm 27:4, "One thing have I asked of the Lord, that will I seek after: that I may dwell in the house of the Lord all the days of my life, to gaze upon the beauty of the Lord and to inquire in his temple." Being busy doing many things can really be a trap that will devastate your life. We can only find our distinction in Christ. Therefore, it is essential to gaze on His face, and listen to His voice leading us.

Rise Up and Possess Our Soul

There has even been many who have become codependent on ministers to find their destiny rather than on the Lord, and it has disrupted God's purpose and empowerment. In this new season many will rise and possess their souls by taking back the fragments of themselves that have been shattered through ungodly soul ties from their past life, but to do that; we must purposefully allow the Lord to take His seat upon the throne of our life, getting our lives prioritized and getting healed in our emotions.

Our greatest enemy will not be demon powers but will be our soulish area, which is our mind, will and our emotions. When we learn to be still, (Psalm 46:10) and watch, and discern, we can hear Gods voice better.

This will be a time to rise up and rule over and possess our own soul. Luke 21:19 (KJV) says, "In your patience possess ye your souls." However, we must quiet our thoughts and silence our feelings, in order to recognize and identify our spiritual atmosphere apart from our soul and be able to move through difficulties with ease. Yet fear often disrupts, when anxiety rules us, and the outcome is always chaos. Isaiah 26:3 says, "You will keep him in perfect peace, whose mind is stayed on You, because he trusts in You." This scripture means when we allow God's peace to rule our hearts; and take dominion over our soul, it's the remedy to overcome fear.

The Holy Spirit will expose things in our soul where we have been bound up. We as a body will purposefully overcome these areas and receive a greater healing than we have ever experienced before. Yet to do that; we will need to possess our soul and allow the Lord to take His seat upon the throne of our soul in order to experience His fullness we've been craving for so long. The result of that will be we'll become strong, healed, fit and emotionally stable.

God will not Release His Blessing Prematurely

God will fulfill His promises, but He will not release His BLESSING prematurely until we are ready for it. Psalms 106:15 says, "And He gave (Israel) them their request; but sent leanness into their soul." The Lord measures us in our soul to see if our character can carry the weight of His blessing. God sometimes must withhold the blessing because our internal world (soulish-realm) is less mature to handle the blessing. Sometimes we miss our chance to see a breakthrough because we aren't praying into His timing or being patient while waiting on the promise. Ecclesiastes 3:1-8 says, "To everything there is a season, and a time to every purpose under the heaven: a time to be born, a time to die; a time to plant, and a time to pluck up that which is planted; a time to kill, and a time to heal; A time to break down, and a time to build up; a time to weep, and a time to laugh; a time to mourn, and a time to dance; a time to cast away stones, and a time to gather stones together; A time to embrace, and a time to refrain from embracing; a time to get, and a time to lose; A time to keep, and a time to cast away; a time to rend, and a time to sew; A time to keep silence, and a time to speak; a time to love, and a time to hate; a time of war, and a time of peace."

As a Father, He measures to see what we can handle responsibly. Even if we are praying out of anxiety, fear, or a slave mentality, instead of a Son or Daughter, then we are not praying out of our identity that brings forth the promise. Therefore, God won't release the blessing prematurely, because we will waste it.

John 19:3-5, 27 says, "To him the doorkeeper opens, and the sheep hear his voice, and he calls his own sheep by name and leads them out. "When he puts forth all his own, he goes ahead of them, and the sheep follow him because they know his voice. "A stranger they simply will not follow, but will flee from him, because they do not know the voice of strangers." "My sheep hear My voice, and I know them, and they follow Me."

A good example of how Jesus carried all authority was that He had confidence in stepping out in doing what He saw His Father doing and saying what He heard His Father saying. Many people today are only doing what they see their spiritual fathers doing traditionally as a hard taskmaster, but they are not modeling an intimate father-son-daughter relationship. Remember, in John 5:19-20 Jesus said, "Truly, truly, I say to you, the Son can do nothing of Himself, unless it is something He sees the Father doing; for whatever the Father does, these things the Son also does in like manner. For the Father loves the Son and shows Him all things that He Himself is doing; and the Father will show Him greater works than these, so that you will marvel."

Walking in the Spirit requires a deep reality of knowing the Father's heart. Walking in the Spirit means 'an anguished longing to experience the deep love of the Father.' God longs to take us into a deeper reality, into His HEART, but we're still carnal or immature.

The 'deeper reality' of the Father's love will refine you from a religious carnality to being a true son of God. We could say that all authentic ministry is about seeing and hearing what God is saying out of an intimate relationship.

Our words reveal to others how we see ourselves, and they also set the tone in the way others will see us. The way you see yourself is the way others will treat you. How we see ourselves reveals how we see our giants and how we will speak to them.

You will either see yourself as a grasshopper or a giant slayer. As we are identifying ourselves as a son of God; we will see from a new perspective to see how God sees things. Then we're empowered to make constant adjustments as we draw close to His heart, then we will step into His purpose. We need to see with our spiritual eyes, similar to the Eagle to see what God is revealing to the TRUE SONS OF GOD. Ephesians 1:17-19 a says, "that the God of our Lord Jesus Christ, the Father of glory, may give you a spirit of wisdom and of revelation in the knowledge of Him.

I pray that the eyes of your heart may be enlightened, so that you will know what is the hope of His calling, what are the riches of the glory of His inheritance in the saints, and what is the boundless greatness of His power toward us who believe."

Give us Eagle Eyes

We need EAGLE EYES that can see keenly from a distance. The eye of the eagle is very keen. The eagle has something like an inner eyelid, only it is very thin; that when needed can draw this over its eye, like a curtain, whenever there is too much light. You have heard perhaps that it can look directly at the bright sun; and there is a reason for that. It can see a great deal farther than we can; and when it is very high in the air, the eagle can see a small animal on the ground; to our eye it would look like a speck, but to the eagle; it clearly observes it and will fly down to catch it. Therefore we must see with our spiritual eyes similar to the Eagle and not our natural eyes.

Elisha saw with the eyes of the Spirit

In the days of the prophet Elisha, there is a story where Elijah saw with the eyes of the Spirit. The king of Syria seized upon an opportunity to capture Elisha

144

who was in the city of Dothan. He mobilized a great army with many chariots and horses to surround the city one night. He wasn't going to risk the prophet escaping from them.

Early the next morning in Dothan, when Elisha's servant went outside, he saw troops, horses, and chariots surrounding them everywhere. He and Elisha were completely surrounded by their enemy forces with the intent on killing them. The servant flew into a state of panic and cried out to Elisha, "Alas, my master! What shall we do?" (2 Kings 6:15).

Put yourself in the shoes of Elisha's servant. You (and I) would probably have been filled with fear too. Without faltering, Elisha calmly told his servant, "Do not fear, for those who are with us are more than those who are with them." (2 Kings 6:16). There was absolutely no logic in what Elisha had just said. I mean think about it, there were just the two of them against a whole army! Had his master gone mad?

2 Kings 6:15-17 says, "When the servant of the man of God got up and went out early the next morning, an army with horses and chariots had surrounded the city. "Oh no, my lord! What shall we do?" the servant

asked. "Don't be afraid," the prophet answered. Before the servant could work himself into an even greater panic, Elisha prayed a simple prayer: "Lord, I pray, open his eyes (the servants) that he may see" (2 Kings 6:17). And the Lord opened the eyes of the servant. "Those who are with us are more than those who are with them." And Elisha prayed, "Open his eyes, Lord, so that he may see." Then the Lord opened the servant's eyes, and when he looked and saw the hills full of magnificent horses and chariots of fire all around them. God's army of angels surrounded them on every side. As the servant marveled, he realized that the Syrian forces were utterly blocked by the angelic army.

Why had the young servant been fearful while Elisha was fearless? The answer is this: They saw different things. The young man saw the great Syrian army with his natural eyes. But Elisha saw an even greater angelic army of chariots of fire with his spiritual eyes. Elisha looked with his spiritual eyes, but the servant didn't.

You see; We need our eyes opened to see how God is working all things together for our good. In the natural things may appear to be unfolding badly, however, God has angels working things around for our good that brings blessing and spiritual advancement. That doesn't mean the situation is any more pleasant, but when you know that God is working in the Spirit, there is a peace and an expectancy for good that comes over you. I will take that any day over stress, anxiety, worry, and panic.

Right now I believe God is doing a spiritual sight correction in many people's eyes. God is going to show us some things that are going to leave us in awe of His goodness. He wants us to rest in the peace of God knowing that even when bad things are happening around us; we are going to experience the tangible and manifested presence of God.

Just as Elisha prayed for the servant's eyes, I too pray that your spiritual eyes would be opened to see beyond the natural realm.

I pray you will see what the enemy doesn't want you to see. I pray you will see with your spiritual eyes to discern the season we're in. I declare it over you now by the authority of Jesus Christ. I also pray as God makes your spiritual sight keener you will allow God to give you deeper revelation that comes through intimacy with Him.

New Speech

To get into your NEW SEASON, you're going to need a NEW SPEECH.

As prophetic carriers of God's glory, we need to have our mouth in alignment with God's plan. God speaks to us in many ways. He can speak to us through HIS WORD, through a prophet, through the spirit of prophecy, through dreams and visions, or BEST; His still small voice, He can give an inner witness, or a prophetic song infusing our inner man. Yet one thing is for sure; all new seasons in our life start with some form of prophetic announcements. The point is this: ONE PROPHETIC ANNOUNCEMENT from the Holy Spirit can launch us into the next season of our life.

Zechariah Lost His Voice

Remember when the Angel of the Lord revealed to Zechariah about the birth of John the Baptist. He told him he would have a son, then told him what his name would be; as well as his destiny. The Spirit prophesied God would use John the Baptist mightily in Luke 1:16-17 saying, "And he will turn many of the sons of Israel back to the Lord their God. And he will go on before the Lord, in the spirit and power of Elijah, to turn the hearts of the parents to their children and the disobedient to the wisdom of the righteous—to make ready a people prepared for the Lord."

After this encounter, Zechariah, John the Baptist father, lost his voice and could not speak until John was born, because the Angel warned him about his doubt and unbelief. Luke 1:20 says, "And behold, you shall be silent and unable to speak until the day when these things take place, because you did not believe my words, which will be fulfilled in their proper time."

Then, right after the birth of John, his father's voice was restored. This is a prophetic sign that we need to take seriously the words we say, to fulfill our destiny.

We are God's Mouthpiece

We should guard all negative talk in our mouth if we want to be God's mouthpiece. We must get in agreement with prophetic words, and own them, if we want them to come to pass.

As a carrier of a prophetic word, when we speak, it should give out light as a burning and shining lamp. Jesus said this in John 5:32 about John the Baptist, "There is another who testifies of Me, and I know that the testimony which He gives about Me is true. You have sent to John, and he has testified to the truth. But the testimony which I receive is not from man, but I say these things so that you may be saved. He (JOHN) was the lamp that was burning and was shining and you will rejoice for a while in his light. But the testimony which I have is greater than the testimony of John; for the works which the Father has given Me to accomplish—the very works that I do—testify about Me, that the Father has sent Me."

John the Baptist said he came to bear witness to the light–but he was not THE LIGHT. Both John and Jesus knew how to stay in alignment with the voice of God. One knew He was THE LIGHT, and the other knew he was a lamp shining the light.

One could say that all prophetic ministry means is to "speak forth the heart of God and communicate a present word of truth." We need the ability to speak present truth meaning we are saying what God is presently saying, as well as purposely NOT speaking negatively.

We must refuse to speak negative words about ourselves but to do that, first we must separate ourselves from all past regret, defeat and disappointments. Those days are past; and you may not always feel hopeful but don't go by your feelings. Catering to bad feelings empowers them to rule over you; what you focus on is empowered but standing our ground by not giving into them starves our doubts and causes them to lose their power over us. You've heard the cliche "Starve your doubts and feed your faith."

When we line up our words with God's WORD then we will LINE UP with HIS WILL. Zechariah 9:12 says, "Return to the fortress, O prisoners of hope; this very day I am declaring that I will restore double to you," says the Lord.

The Word Being Made Flesh in us

In the beginning God announced the Word was being made flesh when Jesus came on the scene, and now the WORD WANTS TO BE QUICKENED OR MADE FLESH IN US. John 1:1-3 says, "In the beginning was the Word, and the Word was with God, and the Word was God. He was in the beginning with God. All things came into being through Him, and apart from Him nothing came into being that has come into being." Therefore we must believe first, then speak and then we will see God's Word come to pass.

Doubting Thomas

We've all heard of a doubting Thomas who was a skeptic as he refused to believe without direct personal experience—which is a reference to the Apostle Thomas, who refused to believe that the resurrected Jesus had appeared to the ten other apostles, until he could see and feel the wounds of Jesus, he said he would NOT BELIEVE. Thomas said, "Unless I see the imprint of nails in His hands and put my finger in the wounds, I will not believe."

We are often just like Thomas, we often want to see proof of what we believe before we will believe. However, that is not how faith works. Faith believes first, speaks and then sees.

We know from this passage (John 20:29) that God reversed the order from our natural senses. Jesus said, "Blessed are they who did not see, and yet they believed."

Faith does not follow our natural senses or our intellect. When we follow our intellect, we will end up in doubt and unbelief. Doubt is a condition that is rooted in our intellect; therefore, we must take a different position. Confession is affirming what we believe. Confession is faith's way of expressing what we believe. It is witnessing a truth that we have embraced in our heart.

Abraham believed God for the promises of God and he did not waver in unbelief. Romans 4:20-21 says, "Yet, with respect to the promise of God, he (Abraham) **did not waver in unbelief** but grew strong in faith, giving glory to God, and being fully assured that what God had promised, He was able also to perform. Therefore, IT WAS ALSO CREDITED TO HIM AS RIGHTEOUSNESS."

We must guard our hearts from unbelief or we won't possess what God has for us. Hebrews 4:1-2 (NAS) "Therefore, let us fear if, while a promise remains of entering His rest, any one of you may seem to have come short of it. For indeed we have had good news preached to us, just as they also; but the word they heard did not profit them, because it was not united by faith in those who heard."

If our belief is wrong, then our thinking will be wrong. If our thinking is wrong, then our speaking will be wrong. All three - believing, thinking and speaking go together and cannot be separated. When we take charge of our emotions, and our thoughts, we'll notice a new vocabulary and a new speech being activated in our mouth.

Luke 21:15 (ESV) says, "For I will give you a mouth of utterance to you and wisdom, which none of your adversaries will be able to withstand or contradict."

2 Corinthians 10:3-6 says, "For though we walk in the flesh, we do not war according to the flesh, for the weapons of our warfare are not of the flesh, but divinely powerful for the destruction of fortresses. We are destroying speculations and every lofty thing raised up against the knowledge of God, and we are taking every thought captive to the obedience of Christ, and we are ready to punish all disobedience, whenever your obedience is complete."

Hebrews 1:1-3 (NIV) says, "Now faith is being sure of what we hope for (confidence) and certain of what we do not see. By faith we understand the universe was formed at God's command, so that what is seen was not made from what was visible."

When we change the way we think, we will change the way we speak. Then our life will start moving in the right direction.

Be A Prisoner of Hope

I want to encourage you to be a prisoner of HOPE. Over the years, I've learned how to lock myself up in a prison of hope, knowing that God has nothing but His BEST planned for me. He has promised me hope in HIS WORD, therefore our hope is the foundation that our faith stands on. That's why we must make a conscious decision to cultivate a lifestyle of hope in our life, and we do that by keeping our eyes on JESUS.

Romans 5:5 says, "Now hope does not disappoint, because the love of God has been poured out in our hearts by the Holy Spirit who was given to us."

Romans 15:13 says, "Now may the God of hope fill you with all joy and peace in believing, so that you will abound in hope by the power of the Holy Spirit."

Unbelief comes is 3 ways:

1. Through wrong knowledge or a wrong belief system; you can't believe something that hasn't been revealed to you. We must seek God for wisdom and ask for His revelation knowledge of the real truth. If your belief system is off base from the truth this will keep you from experiencing what God wants you to have.

2. Through natural unbelief or even through the way others are telling you to believe, like doctors, family or friends. Doctors aren't always wrong, and we should weigh what they are saying but if we are totally relying only on what the doctor says, what the news says, or what our friends and family are saying, etc., we can be influenced in a wrong direction.

3. Through a hardened heart. We are called to stand out and believe for the impossible and depend on God and not the philosophy of the world's system.

Therefore it's crucial we don't allow unbelief into our heart because we won't receive the promises of God.

As we learn to bind up speculations and take every negative thought captive that is in disobedience to the Word of God, speaking God's Word becomes easier and easier.

God has given us His Word to get our believing, our thinking and our mouth in sync together.

Our Tongue will Steer Our Destiny

Our tongue steers us into our destiny. As we begin to think on a higher level, and build a platform on what God says, then we will start to speak new things, and steer our destiny through our new speech, that's in agreement with what God says, then it will manifest.

James 3:4-11 says, "Look at the ships also, though they are so great and are driven by strong winds, are still directed by a very small rudder wherever the inclination of the pilot desires. So also the tongue is a small part of the body, and yet it boasts of great things. See how great a forest is set aflame by such a small fire! And the tongue is a fire, the very world of iniquity; the tongue is set among our members as that which defiles the entire body, and sets on fire the course of our life, and is set on fire by hell. For every species of beasts and birds, of reptiles and creatures of the sea, is tamed and has been tamed by the human race. But no one can tame the tongue; it is a restless evil and full of deadly poison. With it we bless our Lord and Father, and with it we curse men, who have been made in the likeness of God; from the same mouth come both blessing and cursing. My brethren, these things ought not to be this way. Does a fountain send out from the same opening both fresh and bitter water?"

Words have Destinations

Whatever controls our tongue, controls our destiny and the only way we can change the course of our life is by changing the words that we speak. Words have destinations. The word 'destination' is firmly tied to the word 'destiny'. Destiny is a place in our future. It is the ultimate end of a determined course, or an expected end. We need to take notice of our words because they are steering our life. If we change our words, we'll change the whole course of our destination.

Romans 10:17 says, "Faith comes from hearing, and hearing by the Word of Christ."

Psalm 119:15-16 says, "I will meditate on Your precepts And regard Your ways. I shall delight in Your statutes; I shall not forget Your Word."

A Seasonal Change

The Word of God is the good seed, our heart is the soil, and our faith will germinate the seed when we get it out of our mouth and in sync with our heart.

Every time there is a seasonal change in our life, our words and expectations are involved. What we think about the most comes to fruition, and especially as we put the power of expectation with it. Joshua 1:8 says, "This book of the law shall not depart from your mouth, but you shall meditate on it day and night, so that you may be careful to do according to all that is written in it; for then you will make your way prosperous, and then you will have success."

The word 'MEDITATE' means to ponder, to plant, and to think deeply. Meditation is a way to plant seeds in our heart and to ponder on the Word of God repeatedly until it's planted deep in our spirit. When we meditate, which means we mull over it again and again, till it becomes a part of us. It's like how a cow chews its cud over and over. Meditation will write God's Word on the tablets of our heart, as we chew on it day and night.

When we speak God's Word, we activate our faith and where we find faith, we will find expectation. Last, where there is expectation, you will find manifestation. Our heart was designed by God to germinate seed. Our words are seeds as we speak them forth through faith. The Apostle Paul wrote that faith and words can be connected in the Spirit. 2 Corinthians 4:13 says, "But having the same spirit of faith, according to what is written, "I BELIEVED, THEREFORE I SPOKE," we also believe; therefore, we also speak." We should want to germinate good seed in the soil of our heart.

To germinate means to produce, make, create, and cause it to grow. Even in the natural, soil grows seed, whether good or bad. Matthew 12:36-37 (NAS) says, "The good person brings out of his good treasure good things; and the evil person brings out of his evil treasure evil things. But I tell you that every **careless** word (KJV uses the word **idle**) that people speak, they shall give an accounting for it in the Day of Judgment. For by your words you will be justified, and by your words you will be condemned."

The word '**idle**' means careless. They are defined as useless, negative, inoperative and nonproductive. Such careless words that we speak are inoperative and nonproductive and, according to Jesus, we will have to give an account for them on the Day of Judgment.

Our idle or careless words have no value because they do not connect to faith!! Isn't it interesting that Jesus does not say we are justified or condemned by our deeds but by our words?

Proverbs 4:23 says, "Watch over your heart with all diligence, for from it flow the springs of life." The truth is that we are employing our words every day in one way or another. In other words, we are getting a paycheck on them. Our words are either making our lives richer or depleting everything that God has promised in His Word.

Our tongue is a powerful weapon and if we want to get to our destiny, we must not let the enemy steal our confession. Jesus is the HIGH PRIESTS of our confession, and He watches and listens over our words to perform it. Hebrews 3:1 says, "Therefore, holy brethren, partakers of a heavenly calling, consider Jesus, the Apostle and High Priest of our confession." Numbers 14:28 (NIV) also confirms this saying, "When God spoke to Moses, so tell them, as surely as I live, declares the LORD, I will do to you the very thing I heard you say."

Our Words get to Our Future before We Do

God does listen to our words, and manifestation is released as we declare God's Word by voice activating it. We must think from the new man, and see through the lens of the new man, then we will start to speak new things. Our words can literally chart a path into our future. I like to say, "Our words get to our future before we do." Every thought that we think, and every word we speak is creating something in our future. If we have been speaking idle, careless, or nonproductive words, we can repent and change our words. Just as Isaiah asked the Lord to take the burning coal from the altar and cleanse his lips, we can ask God to cleanse our lips, and change what our tongues have been proclaiming. (Isaiah 6: 5-7)

Therefore, speaking to mountains is faith in action. The mountains you see are never bigger than the God we serve. Mark 11:23 says, "Truly I say to you, whoever says to this mountain, 'Be taken up and cast into the sea,' and does not doubt in his heart, but believes that what he says is going to happen, it will be granted him."

The Woman with the Issue of Blood

We see another example of the power of words through the woman with the issue of blood, and how she framed her healing. If God framed His world through words, then so should we. Hebrews 1:1-3 says, "Now faith is the assurance of things hoped for, the conviction of things not seen. For by it the men of old gained approval. By faith we understand that the worlds were prepared by the word of God, so that what is seen was not made out of things which are visible. All things were made by Him; and without Him nothing was made or framed."

The woman with the issue of blood certainly framed her world with God's covenant Word. She planted a healing seed in her heart. Matthew 9: 21-22 says, For she was saying to herself, "If I only touch His garment, I will get well." Jesus turning to her, said,

"Daughter, take courage; your faith has made you well." And at once the woman was made well.

- She planted words in her heart. (She said to herself.)

- She decreed how and when she would receive. (When touching His garment.)

- Her heart germinated a miracle of healing in her body. ("Your faith has made you well.")

What is a Decree

A definition of a biblical decree is an official order issued by a legal authority. A decree is taking Gods words and speaking it out. We have been given the authority from Jesus to make these decrees into our realms of influence and as we do, it will begin to create the will of God in our life in the spiritual realm.

Historically, in God's WORD, only a king could make a decree. Job 22:28-29 says, "You will also decree a thing, and it will be established for you; and light will shine on your ways. When you are cast down, you will speak with confidence, and the humble person He will save."

The Hebrew word for 'decree' in this passage is 'gazar' which is a command that not only establishes something but also cuts and divides something down that is in OPPOSITION TO GOD's plan, which brings me to a confrontation of evil.

Confrontation from Ahab had Jezebel

Remember Ahab married Jezebel whose father was the high priest of Ashtaroth, who built a temple to a false God named Baal who walked in the sins of Jeroboam and installed people in ministry who were not called by God. Elijah had a confrontation with King Ahab where he made a powerful decree.

1 Kings 17:1 says, "Now Elijah the Tishbite, who was of the settlers of Gilead, said to Ahab, "As the LORD, the God of Israel lives, before whom I stand, surely there shall be neither dew nor rain these years, **except by my word.**" Elijah was bold in declaring to Ahab that it would not rain again until he said it would rain. He said it would not rain "**except by my word.**"

And guess what? It didn't.

Decree's Unlock Doors given by Jesus to the Ekklesia

Mature Sons understand their God-given authority to decree a thing, to unlock and open doors. As we discover and use our authority as a king, we can decree a thing, and it will be established. This is a tremendous promise.

Decrees are like arrows being released from our mouths, piercing and penetrating the atmosphere. Decrees open portals and gateways in the spiritual realm. Negative decrees have the power to dam up or block the flow of God in our life. But as mature Sons of God, we know a decree is a legally binding command we can release however it must be led by the Spirit. Romans 8:14 says, "For all who are being led by the Spirit of God, these are sons of God."

Some doors in our life are shut and some are locked. Seeing a locked door is proof that a key is needed and that a key exists. Therefore, when we quote God's WORD, there is much power made available to unlock those doors through the key of faith.

We have the power to bind satanic activity in Jesus' Name on the earth and God will back us up, but we must decree it through our identity.

Jesus Christ gave His Ekklesia authority to bind and loose with the authority of our mouth. Jesus said, "I will give you the keys of the kingdom of heaven; and whatever you bind on earth shall have been bound in heaven, and whatever you loose on earth shall have been loosed in heaven." Matthew 16: 19 says, "Again, I say to you, that if two of you agree on earth about anything that they may ask, it shall be done for them by My Father who is in heaven. For where two or three have gathered together in My name, I am there in their midst."

The Greek text of Matthew 18: 20 says, "I am there to make good that which they agree on." We could say it another way, whatsoever we forbid shall be forbidden and whatsoever we allow shall be allowed. Now, that's delegated authority sent as a command by a king. From the text of God's Word, we are a priest and a king who's been given delegated authority. 1 Peter 2:9 says that we are a royal priesthood (A kingdom of priest) and Revelation 1:6

says that Christ has "made us kings and priests unto God."

God is shaking us to RISE UP in HIS strength. When the BRIDE of CHRIST realizes her delegated authority, she will be bolder than a lion. Proverbs 28: 1b says, "...the righteous are bold as a lion."

We will have more confidence than a lion because JESUS is our confidence. When God speaks in His LION voice, it will penetrate DEEP INTO the hearts of HIS people; and it will be a voice that will OPEN our hearts for what He's preparing us for. Isaiah 42:13 says, "The LORD will go forth like a warrior; He will arouse His zeal like a man of war. He will utter a shout, yes; He will raise a war cry. He will prevail against His enemies."

The Lord's VOICE will penetrate so deep that we will not shrink back in the day of battle because our confidence is in our God. The Lord is calling us OUT TO BE AS BOLD LIONS to send it forth with a command because the Lion of Judah lives on the inside of us.

The word 'Command' means 'to charge or to enjoin ourselves in agreement until it comes to pass.' We have to take an aggressive posture, and not say, "Well, I guess if God wants me to have it, He'll make it happen. Whatever will be will be?" No, don't buy into the Doris Day syndrome. IT'S NOT KE SERA, WHATEVER WILL BE, WILL BE.

The mystery of speaking, decreeing and declaring, is a part of the spiritual warfare. That's why we must contend for the promise by breaking through every demonic attack of fear, doubt, confusion, vain imaginations, and unbelief.

There are Word Thieves

There are 'Word Thieves' that will try to steal the promises of God in our life. God gives us the authorization to make a binding command as kings and it will come to pass. However if our identity isn't aligned TO THE LORD, as a son of God and seeing HIM as Father and our king, then we can't receive the promise. We need to find the battle words that God wants us to speak and use them against the enemy. That is called 'Contending for the Promise!"

Every prophetic word we get from God will experience warfare, and you will need to contend for the promise. Timothy was Paul's spiritual son and he encouraged him to fight the good fight of faith in accordance with the prophesies that were previously made concerning him. 1Timothy 1:18 says, "This command I entrust to you, Timothy, my son, in accordance with the prophecies previously made concerning you, that by them you fight the good fight." In other words; He was saying, "Send it with a command."

Timothy had some fear and insecurity that he needed to overcome. If we will get our speech in alignment with God's Word, the timidity and fearfulness will come off of us, and God will awaken His PROPHETIC WORDS THROUGH OUR MOUTH.

Yes, there is dominion in our tongues, and our tongues release our faith through our words. God wants to awaken the Lion in us, but we must know our identity in Him. Amos 3:7-8 says, "The lion has roared; who will not fear? The Lord God has spoken; who can but prophesy?"

When we start speaking, decreeing and declaring, several thieves will attack including demonic spirits, fear, doubt, confusion, vain imaginations, and unbelief. Words have the power of life and death.

Words are involved in every new season in our life. Some words make us feel terrific and other words can make us feel terrible. Words that are fearful, or angry or even death words can devastate us. Proverbs 18:21 says, "Death and life are in the power of the tongue, and those who love it will eat its fruit."

We need to be ready with battle words inside of us given by the Spirit to stop demonic influences and prepare for what is coming by using the keys of the Kingdom. Remember when the Spirit led Jesus into the wilderness to be tempted by the devil, Jesus had battle words ready for Satan. Each time Jesus was challenged by Satan, He responded with; "It is written."

Thinking like a son of God, will cause us to speak like an over comer. We are not fighting **for the victory**, we are fighting **from the victory** and **from the identity of Sonship and Bride ship**. When we learn to live from Christ, we will become as we see Him. However, if we live for God, instead of from God, we will live as an achiever instead of a receiver. We must not forget in our relationship with the Lord, **He**

partners with our new identity and reveals revelation through the NEW LENS of our NEW MAN.

The only reason the battle still rages inside of us is because we haven't yet learned to "think like a son of God." We no longer have to view our circumstances through the lens of our old man or through "the natural mind." Instead, we are learning to walk with the **new lens of the Kingdom.**

Once our identity lines up as a son of God then our words will line up and we'll see the promises of God manifest. However, we must learn to get in proper alignment with our identity as a son of God (not gender; put positionally knowing who we are in Christ) then we can decree it, give breath to it, say it out loud, and declare it to be so, and the promise will manifest. This proves knowing the LION OF JUDAH lives inside of us, when we are bold, HE WILL ROAR THROUGH US!!!

The following statements are some VERBAL DECREE'S we can make as a TRUE SON OF GOD:

I DECREE the keys of the kingdom of heaven have been given to me, and whatsoever I bind on earth is bound in heaven and whatsoever I loose on earth is loosed in heaven. (Matthew 16:19)

I DECREE no weapon formed against me shall prosper, and every tongue that shall rise against me in judgment shall be condemned. (Isaiah 54:17)

I DECREE I am blessed coming in and blessed going out. I am the head and not the tail, above only, and not beneath. (Deuteronomy 28:13)

I DECREE I am strong in the Lord and the power of His might as I put on the whole armor of God and stand against all the wiles of the devil. (Ephesians 6:11)

I DECREE my steps are ordered every day by the Lord. (Psalm 37:23)

I DECREE all things work together for my good because I love God and I am called according to His purpose. (Romans 8:28)

I DECREE God is my refuge and strength, a very present help in times of trouble. (Psalms 46:1)

I DECREE God has not given me the spirit of fear, but of power, love, and a sound mind. (2 Timothy 1:7)

I DECREE the LORD renews my strength; I mount up with wings as eagles; I run, and shall not be weary, walk, and will not faint. (Isaiah 40:31)

I DECREE the favor of God. If God be for me, who can be against me? (Romans 8:31)

I DECREE I give and it shall be given back to me; good measure, pressed down, shaken together, and running over, shall men give into my bosom. (Luke 6:38)

I DECREE I delight myself in the LORD and He gives me the desires of my heart. (Psalms 37:4)

I DECREE I have the peace of God that passes all understanding. (Philippians 4:7)

I DECREE I am a believer with signs that follow me. In the Name of Jesus, I cast out devils, speak with new tongues, take up serpents, and if I drink any deadly thing it will not harm me; I lay hands on the sick, and they will recover. (Mark 16:17-19)

I DECREE greater is He that lives in me than he that lives in the world. (1 John 4:4)

I DECREE My God supplies all my needs according to His riches in glory by Christ Jesus. (Philippians 4:19)

I DECREE by His stripes; I am healed. (1 Peter 2:24)

I DECREE I am born of God, and the evil one cannot touch me. (1 John 5:18)

I DECREE I call on the Lord and He answers me and shows me great and mighty things I know not of. (Jeremiah 33:3)

I DECREE I have been given the power to tread on serpents and scorpions, and over all the power of the enemy: and nothing shall by any means hurt me. (Luke 10:19)

I DECREE God gives me the treasures of darkness and hidden riches of secret places that I may know that the LORD is God. (Isaiah 45:3)

I DECREE God is not a man that He should lie to me, neither the son of man that he should change His mind. The things He has said, He will do, and the things He has spoken He will make good. (Numbers 23:19)

I DECREE that the battle will not rage between my soul and spirit inside of me, bringing my soul and spirit together in union with the Father's will causing me to 'think like a son of God.' I will no longer be fragmented like an orphan without a father. (Romans 8:15-17)

I DECREE wealth and riches shall be in my house because I fear the Lord. (Psalm 112:3)

I DECREE the kingdom of God to come in my life, family, marriage, ministry, relationships, and at work. (Matthew 6:10)

I DECREE I am satisfied with the words of my mouth because life and death are in the power of my tongue. (Proverbs 18:20)

I DECREE new warfare strategies in my life; strategies that come from the Fathers heart as I partner with Him in every battle creating a Kingdom Revolution in my life. (2 Corinthians 2:10-12)

I DECREE that the sins on my family bloodline are redeemed from every generational curse. I cancel every bloodline curse that has come through the sins of my forefathers to the 3rd and 4th generations past, I decree and appropriate the power of the Blood of Jesus. I decree every generational curse is cut off of my bloodline in Jesus Name. (Duet.5:9)

I DECREE that all distractions will not hinder God's will for my life. I will submit myself in total surrender and I will be attentive to His VOICE, and not be distracted. (Proverbs 2:2-6)

I DECREE that a new sound will come out of me to unify with the body of Christ corporately. (Psalm 133:1-3)

Therefore this brings us to another important truth in the teaching that there will be a new sound and a new song of unity helping us to form new and healthy relationships.

New Sound and A New Song of Unity

There will be NEW SOUNDS & NEW SONGS of unity in this next prophetic move.

To get into our NEW season; we must flow corporately. In the scriptures, KINGS KNEW WHEN TO GO TO WAR in the SPRING OF THE YEAR, and they knew they had to fight corporately. Jesus prayed in John 17 that the corporate body would become ONE, and yet we have seen so much division in the Body of Christ. Therefore, until we can get unified and love each other, we can't win the world for Jesus.

Colossians 3:16 in the Passion Translation says, "Let the WORD of CHRIST live in you richly, flooding you with all wisdom. Apply the Scriptures as you teach and instruct one another with the Psalms, and festive praise, and with prophetic songs given spontaneously by the Spirit."

Psalm 42:7 says, "Deep calls to deep at the sound of Your waterfalls; All Your breakers and Your waves have rolled over me."

God is trying to get our attention to usher in a NEW SOUND FROM HEAVEN, but we're distracted. The enemy designed the enticements of this lower world, and its charms to draw our hearts away from Christ. We should be concerned about how worthy HE is OF OUR DEVOTION TO HIM and NO MATTER WHAT WE MUST BE DETERMINED NOT TO BE DISTRACTED BY ANYTHING.

We are living in a time that heaven wants to release a NEW SOUND AND A NEW SONG FROM HEAVEN, but we're not listening because we are NOT UNIFIED.

The Father IS CALLING THE REMNANT AS ONE CORPORATE NEW MAN TO ARISE BLOWING THE SOUND OF A UNIFIED BODY THAT IS PROCLAIMING

A KINGDOM REVOLUTION IN THE EARTH. We are warriors that sit in heavenly places together. (Ephesians 2:6) We cannot win the corporate battle until THE CORPORATE MATURED SONS ARE UNIFIED. We MUST NOT WORK independently, but working together through a supply that comes out of unity is what will take THE ENEMY DOWN to accomplish God's 'GREATER PLAN.'

Our sound won't be heard to pull the enemy's camp down until we are unified. God is bringing forth a new sound of unity through HIS PEOPLE, If we want to see this next generation reached for Jesus, two things must happen.

1. We must be FITTED TOGETHER CORPORATELY, working together in unity.

2. We must love and honor each other.

In John 17:21, Jesus prayed His High Priestly prayer as He prayed to the Father, "... that they all may be one; even as You, Father, are in Me and I in You, that they may also be in Us, so that the world may believe that You sent Me."

John 13:34-35 says, "A new commandment I give to you, that you love one another, even as I have loved you, that you also love one another. By this all men will know that you are My disciples, if you have love for one another."

God is positioning us to hear the sound of HIS GLORY!

God's sound is positioning us to hear the sound of HIS GLORY breaking through religious stronghold and barriers. We are moving into a NEW and unprecedented season unlike we've never seen before. We must be mindful of this sound, so that we can manifest the glory of God. The SOUND OF UNITY sounds like the voice of many waters coming into the earth. Ezekiel 42:2 says, "Behold, the glory of the God of Israel was coming from the way of the east. And His voice was like the sound of many waters; and the earth shone with His glory."

Psalm 29:3-4; 8-11 says, "The voice of the LORD is over the waters; THE GOD OF GLORY thunders; The LORD is over many waters. The voice of the LORD is powerful; The voice of the LORD is full of majesty. The voice of the LORD shakes the wilderness; the LORD shakes the Wilderness of Kadesh. The voice of the LORD makes the deer gives birth and strips the forest bare; AND IN HIS TEMPLE EVERYONE SAY, "GLORY! The LORD sat enthroned at the Flood, and the LORD sits as King forever. The LORD will give strength to His people; The LORD will bless His people with peace."

Nehemiah's Refused TO BE Distracted

As you read through the story of Nehemiah, one thing you will notice is the enemy came in through the open door of distraction. Nehemiah 6:1-15 says, "Now when it was reported to Sanballat, Tobiah, to Geshem the Arab and to the rest of our enemies that I had rebuilt the wall, and that no breach remained in it, although at that time I had not set up the doors in the gates, then Sanballat and Geshem sent a message to me, saying, "Come, let us meet together at Chephirim in the plain of Ono." But they were planning to harm me. So, I sent messengers to them, saying, "I am doing a great work and I cannot come down. Why should the work stop while I leave it and come down to you?" They sent messages to me four times in this manner, and I answered them in the same way. Then Sanballat sent his servant to me in the same manner a fifth time with an open letter in his hand. In it was written, "It is reported among the nations, and Gashmu says, that you and the Jews are planning to rebel; therefore, you are rebuilding the wall. And you are to be their king, according to these reports. "You have also appointed prophets to proclaim in Jerusalem concerning you, 'A king is in Judah!' And now it will be reported to the king according to these reports. So come now, let us take counsel together." Then I sent a message to him saying, "Such things as you are saying have not been done, but you are inventing them in your own mind." For all of them were trying to frighten us, thinking, "They will become discouraged with the work and it will not be done." But now, O God, strengthen my hands. When I entered the house of Shemaiah the son of Delaiah, son of Mehetabel, who was confined at home, he said, "Let us meet together in the house of God, within the temple, and let us close the doors of the temple, for they are coming to kill you, and they are coming to kill you at night." But I said, "Should a man like me flee? And could one such as I go into the temple to save his life? I will not go in." Then I perceived that surely God had not sent him, but he uttered his prophecy against me because

Tobiah and Sanballat had hired him. He was hired for this reason, that I might become frightened and act accordingly and sin, so that they might have an evil report in order that they could reproach me. Remember, O my God, Tobiah and Sanballat according to these works of theirs, and also Noadiah the prophetess and the rest of the prophets who were trying to frighten me. So the wall was completed on the twenty-fifth of the month Elul, in fifty-two days."

The enemy has many tactics to prevent us from stepping into our destiny, and one of those tactics is distraction. Distraction is sent to draw us away from our God-given assignment, and the enemy uses it as a decoy to interrupt the flow of the Holy Spirit in our lives. Distraction can be described as mental distress, a diversion sent to lead us off course, to delay the fulfillment of our prophetic promises. A spirit of distraction has one primary intent, and that is to hinder!

In Nehemiah Chapter 6, Nehemiah had finished the wall of Jerusalem except for installing the doors to the gates of the city. When the enemies of Judah realized Nehemiah had completed the restoration process, they plotted against Nehemiah to stop his progress. Judah's enemies–Sanballat, Tobiah, and Geshem–devised evil schemes to hinder Nehemiah through distraction, conspiracy, and even physical threats. A great and effective door had opened to Nehemiah to re-establish the city of Jerusalem; however, it wasn't without opposition.

Sometimes, when a door of breakthrough is before us, the enemy threatens to come in behind us, to draw us off course. We've been given powerful tools of spiritual warfare, but we must be attentive to His VOICE, and not be distracted.

When Nehemiah faced the opposition from his adversaries, he discerned the strategy of the enemy and avoided being drawn into the snare of verbal discourse, accusation and distraction. Nehemiah recognized the decoy of distraction sent by the enemy to halt and hinder his progress!

Therefore, Nehemiah didn't engage in any verbal dispute with his enemies because he believed that God was for him. Romans 8:31 says, "What then shall we say to these things? If God is for us, who is against us?"

Nehemiah used wisdom and undistracted focus to defeat the foe before him. Even when Tobiah, Sanballat and Geshem, (which represents carnal thinking and the ways of the world) rose up as his adversarial cohorts, yet Nehemiah didn't fall prey to the stress and pressure to perform to their demands. Never forget; this will always be a test of every believer. Now let's move to the next step which is learning new spiritual warfare strategies from the Lord.

New Spiritual Warfare Strategies

There's an onslaught of ATTACK as the enemy is coming against people's minds, their marriages, their families, and their bodies. Therefore, the Lord is calling HIS WARRIORS TO RECEIVE NEW STRATEGIES that resemble military training.

There will be NEW SPIRITUAL WARFARE STRATEGIES in this next prophetic move to prepare us for what's ahead.

To get into your NEW SEASON, you're going to need NEW STRATEGIES OF SPIRITUAL WARFARE.

The Lord is going to do the following as we partner with Him; He says:

- I will teach you how to fight at this NEW level in unity and maturity.

- I will teach you how to think, walk, talk, fight, strategize, hear My voice, and go to war with new warfare strategies.

- I will teach you new depths in the Spirit that will bring you into new revelation, new praise, new worship, new warfare, new love, and new power.

- I will teach and train you how to be a warrior with my end-time weapons.

Ai was a Painful Place

REMEMBER the battles that Joshua faced; after, he lost the battle at Ai. Joshua 8:18 says, "I am about to bring a victory in the very place you suffered defeat. Point your spear, your weapon of warfare toward the place of ruin. I will give it to you in TOTAL TRIUMPH!"

In fact, God saved us, so we could overcome the world. In I John 5; 4 it says, "For whatever is born of God overcomes the world; and this is the victory that has overcome the world--our faith." This is not just faith that believes that Jesus saves but faith that joins with Him ruling in victory as A KINGDOM REVOLUTION.

We are a KINGDOM OF PRIEST advancing Christ's kingly reign in our life. Therefore we are not called to escape our battles, but to rule over them.

John 16:33 says, "These things I have spoken to you, so that in Me you may have peace. In the world you have tribulation but take courage; I have overcome the world."

The Amplified Version of John 16:33 says, "In the world you will have tribulation and trials and distress, and frustration; but be of good cheer [take courage; be confident, certain, undaunted]! I have overcome the world. [I have deprived it of power to harm and conquered for you.]"

Ai was a VERY painful place for Joshua. After the victory and fall of the walls in Jericho, he suffered agonizing defeat in Ai. Disobedience, deception and dishonor had come upon the camp. He faced total defeat, and almost couldn't push forward. The name Ai in Hebrew means 'ruin' and 'kindred root'.

Even Abraham had pitched his tent and built an altar of worship between Bethel (the house of God) and Ai (ruin). Ai represents kindred roots in our family bloodline that need to be broken in prayer. The kindred roots are those generational sins that show up in our family bloodline. They are often rooted in iniquity and transgression, and a propensity toward the sins on our family bloodline. Yet we know we have authority to break out even through those generational strongholds.

Ruby Fiery Kinglet Bird

I have a bird story to tell you. One day a fiery red beautiful bird kept showing up at my window. The bird had a tiny body with a grey and a fiery red crown on its head. I looked it up on google and learned it was a Ruby-Crowned Kinglet Bird. They seemingly only show up in spring and summer, but this one came in January. They are full of energy, forging from branch to branch, flicking their wings from tree to tree.

This bird would come to my window as I would drink my coffee in the mornings. He would just flutter, look at me, and knock on my window with his beak. He captured my attention and was ever so darling. I kept wondering if there was a prophetic meaning to him showing up. I said, "Lord, if You're trying to tell me something; speak Lord, your daughter is listening!"

The Lord spoke to me that the bird represented ruling and reigning with Him. Then that same week, I read a prophecy from a prophetic voice that I admire about firebirds. The prophecy said, The Lord took them into the throne room of heaven. The Lord's throne was arrayed in God's glory, where they saw the Lord's arm resting on the arm of His throne. It was the most beautiful throne where they saw all of the King's magnificence and glory. Then they said they saw firebirds flying all around God's throne. They were radiant with red and gold fire and glory on their heads.

This seemed to line up with the fiery Ruby-Crowned Kinglet Bird that fluttered at my window. Isaiah reminds us also of the fiery Seraphim Angels that were flying in close proximity around the throne, that took on the same glory and fire that was on the King and in exchange was released to them to release it into the earth. (Isaiah 6) Everything that was in proximity to the King and His throne reflected His glory around them and in them.

The Lord spoke to Me saying, "I'm releasing MY FIREBIRDS that have fluttered around my throne in worship to Me, and they that have partaken of MY VERY LIKENESS to reflect MY GLORY will release fire in the earth."

The Lord is drawing HIS PEOPLE TO SET HIS KINGDOM UP INSIDE OF US, where HIS LORDSHIP is ruling through His people. So, we can see as part of our priesthood and kingly anointing for this hour, is that we must rule and reign with JESUS. This is our portion and our inheritance, as we are a "kingdom of priest" destined to reign with Jesus.

The Lord showed me MANY in the body of Christ who have walked through incredibly difficult times, some of the darkest, hardest, fiery seasons they've ever experienced. Yet God is preparing a NEW BREED OF PEOPLE for greater works.

John 14:12-14 says, "Truly, truly, I say to you, he who believes in Me, the works that I do, he will do also; and greater works than these he will do; because I go to the Father. Whatever you ask in My name, that will

I do, so that the Father may be glorified in the Son. If you ask Me anything in My name, I will do it."

Therefore, we are headed for greater things; because the greater ONE lives in us. God is baptizing us with fire and commissioning many of His people from HIS throne room. We are part of a priesthood of kings called to restore and advance the Kingdom of God. Not only was Jesus the Lamb of God who took away the sins of the world, He was also the Restoring King who would perfect His followers for the ruling and reigning as kings with Him.

The Lord is releasing a new breed of people who will carry His fire and His glory, because they have been baptized in the fire of HIS LOVE AND POWER. They have been through the refiner's fire to get the impurities out of them. A baptism of fire represents the old fading away and the new coming forth. Fire is going to be placed upon our heads again, like the Ruby-Crowned Kinglet Bird that visited me. In other words, Christ launched a Kingdom Revolution. This movement was about joining Him in restoring the rule of God on the earth through his covenant people known as the sons of God.

In our fight against the enemy, we must learn to be intentional toward opening our heart to God's love. There is a significant shift of deliverance that is going to catapult God's people into a deeper freedom and joy like we have never known before.

We need a fresh baptism of THE FIRE OF GOD's love to purge out the strongholds of fear, anxiety, terror, torment and chaos. The Lord promises us in His Word, He will never leave nor forsake us, even if we might face some deep waters or we walk through some fiery trials that would try to devour (Isa. 43:2) us in a negative way, we will not be harmed.

Training for Reigning

This is our new season, where we are training for reigning and moving into a higher dimension of spiritual maturity. Our lives have many seasons. We all have seasons of preparation, seasons of silence, of waiting on the Lord, of learning, of letting go, but then, there are seasons of possessing the promises of God.

Philippians 3:8-14 says, "More than that, I count all things to be loss in view of the surpassing value of knowing Christ Jesus my Lord, for whom I have suffered the loss of all things, and count them but rubbish so that I may gain Christ, and may be found in Him, not having a righteousness of my own derived from the Law, but that which is through faith in Christ, the righteousness which comes from God on the basis of faith, that I may know Him and the power of His resurrection and the fellowship of His sufferings, being conformed to His death; in order that I may attain to the resurrection from the dead. Not that I have already obtained it or have already become perfect, but I press on so that I may lay hold of that for which also I was laid hold of by Christ Jesus. Brethren, I do not regard myself as having laid hold of it yet; but one thing I do: forgetting what lies behind and reaching forward to what lies ahead, I press on toward the goal for the prize of the upward call of God in Christ Jesus."

This training ground that we're standing on now must be conquered before we can run with the horses. Jeremiah 12:5 says, "If you have run with the footmen, and they have wearied you, Then how can you contend with horses? And if in the land of peace, In which you trusted, they wearied you, then how will you do in the floodplain of the Jordan?" This is how

God uses a new season, to take us to better places because He knows if we stay where we're at, we will NEVER TAKE HIGHER GROUND.

We are being suited up for the battle. And yes we're living in a critical time that we must be keenly aware and alert to what God desires to accomplish through His people. The Lord is challenging us to come up higher but we must train for it.

1 Corinthians 9:24-27 says, "Do you not know that those who run in a race all run, but only one receives the prize? Run in such a way that you may win. Everyone who competes in the games exercises self-control in all things. They do it to receive a perishable wreath, but we an imperishable. Therefore, I run in such a way, as not without aim; I box in such a way, as not beating the air; but I discipline my body and make it my slave, so that, after I have preached to others, I myself will not be disqualified."

We're Being Trained for Discipline in Our Calling

Paul used an analogy about how to train ourselves for the prize in Christ Jesus. He draws an analogy to a contest they played every two years near Corinth, where people came together to compete in races to win a wreath (prize). Paul said he beat his body, or he brought it under subjection, so that after he had preached to others not practicing the discipline that God required of him, lest he become disqualified.

Did you know you can't fulfill your calling in your comfort zone? As your opportunities increase, so will the opposition. Many people give up when the opposition starts and say what's the use? If God really wanted me to have it, He wouldn't allow this opposition in my life. Really?

We often think if God wanted me to have this—He would stop the enemy. We think, "This is just too hard," and then we walk away. We want to take the path of the least resistance. No, we must contend in the faith- What does it mean to contend? Jude, the half-brother of Jesus, wrote in Jude 1:3 that we would earnestly contend for the faith. The word 'contend' means to push through or to earnestly agonize for our inheritance.

We are being trained for discipline and winning the victory, and yet we often feel hindered and challenged, making it difficult to accomplish what God has called us to do. It is important, however, to realize and understand when believing and contending for supernatural advancement that conflict will come. The permission, the promotion, and the forward progress that many of us are pressing into, often comes where our 'current circumstances' seem to contradict the very thing that God has previously promised us. However, this is also the case with just about every prophetic promise found in God's Word.

We can all look around and see there is still land we haven't taken for God yet. There are still promises we need to possess, but there are some things within our hearts that the Lord wants us to let go of. There are some challenges we will face until we surrender those things to Him.

Never forget that the OPEN DOOR comes with tension and even perceived resistance, that we are called to 'act on' and move forward as God permits. The Lord doesn't want us to fold under pressure, so He trains us through opposition to push us out of our comfort zones. Yes even in 'hard places' we can swim against the current and still be in God's perfect plan.

Remember, where the Lord opens an effectual door, there are many adversaries. 1 Corinthians 16:9 says, "A great and effective door has been opened to me and there are many adversaries." We must keep in mind, the attack is always proportional to the REWARD THAT'S COMING. Therefore stay focused to prepare for the new season regardless of the attacks. God will reward your faithfulness.

New Season (New Structure)

To be prophetic is to declare that one (era) season is finished, and another one has begun.

To get into your NEW SEASON, you're going to need to experience the glory of God that doesn't follow the 'status quo' but it goes against the flow of the 'structured church.'

Once we're called up higher, all the endurance training we went through has only qualified us to withstand, so that God will can take us higher than we've ever been before.

What do I mean by this? The prophetic does not come from the 'status quo.' That means that it is outside the normal place or status quo where most of the Church is. Why is this?

I believe it is because the prophetic must come from a place where there has been a significant break from what the familiar is. That is why it doesn't flow where the structured or traditional church is. Therefore God calls us out of 'structured church or mechanical religion.'

Jack Frost

If you know anything about Jack Frost, and how his ministry went through a 'rupture' before he learned about the 'orphan heart' and being set free and moving into Sonship. His ministry emerged from the desert. The prophetic does not have a central place within the normal life of the institutional Church. It is radically free from the institution and the management and mechanical structure, from the accepted norm.

In the scriptures, you find the prophetic move of God always comes out of the wilderness. Moses, John the Baptist and Jesus' ministry all came out of the wilderness. The prophetic brings a rupture in continuity, which represents a place in the wilderness or the desert where the usual comforts cease. The desert is a place where cultural noise is silenced, and it has stripped cultural trappings bare, and from a significant rupture in the normal way of doing Christianity and church. This is why most of the church is stuck in status quo because they flow with manmade religion and not the prophetic to move with the Holy Spirit. When everything is mechanical in the church; it hinders the move of God. Therefore stay in a place where the Spirit is allowed to move. It's a form of idolatry to manufacture ministry. Therefore stay authentic in your walk with God.

Don't Manufacture Ministry

The Lord is calling His people to stop trying to MANUFACTURE ministry. Purity does not exist where there is manufacturing. Anywhere there is a manufacturing of ministry; there will be self promotion, striving in the flesh, and an unholy mixture. God deliver us from this unholy mixture!

The Father is going to restore us back into a fresh move of HIS SPIRIT BEING POURED OUT ON ALL MANKIND. Joel 2:28-32 says, "It will come about after this that I will pour out My Spirit on all mankind; and your sons and your daughters will prophesy, your old men will have dreams, your young men will see visions. And even on the male and female servants I will pour out My Spirit in those days."

Therefore, it's very important NOT TO MOVE AHEAD OF GOD. Be steadfast in Him and allow yourself to be focused on what He is doing and not be distracted by what others are doing. If doors seemed to have opened and then they slam shut; let me assure you, this is the Lord. These doors closed purposely to protect you. God has prepared you for the seasons to come. And He is working it all out for your good. (Romans 8:28)

There have been so many who are ambitious for ministry, however, if we move out into ministry prematurely and try to open our own doors, and put ourselves in the limelight, it will go sour. God has chosen the foolish things of the world to confound the wise, and the things which are nothing to crush man's pride in those things he has built himself. (1 Corinthians 1:27)

An Exit Door

The Lord is calling us to **exit the door on the old chapter,** so we can step into the new chapter. God showed me we will walk into an exit door before He will bring us into the new door in order to experience THE FULLNESS of Restoration; He longs to bring fullness of restoration of all that was lost in every area of our life. Fullness means 'All Encompassing.' A lot of us have experienced a lot of turbulence; and yes, it's been quite unsettling. But the Lord has been preparing us to walk through an exit door, forgetting those things that are behind and pressing toward the goal of the prize of the upward call of God in Christ Jesus. Philippians 3:13-14 says, "Brethren, I do not regard myself as having laid hold of it yet; but one thing I do: forgetting what lies behind and reaching forward to what lies ahead, I press on toward the goal for the prize of the upward call of God in Christ Jesus."

One day, I probably had the worst day I've ever had, focusing on things that have totally drained my strength. And when I woke up the next day, the Lord said to me, "Say goodbye to the past and hello to the future!"

So, I studied the word 'Forgetting' in Philippians 3:13. To my amazement, in the Greek FORGETTING, is 'epilanthano' which has two compound words 'Epi' and 'lanthano' and it means this: it translates into closing a door in order to walk through a new door. It means something is finished, done with, no longer applicable or obsolete. It may have been true in the past, but it's no longer relevant TODAY. That was encouraging to me because we must exit one door to step into another and forget about what is behind us.

The King of Glory is looking for hearts who are ready; their lamps are full of oil and they've trimmed their wicks. He's looking for those who aren't looking to borrow oil from others, but they have a desire to cultivate an intimate relationship with Him and Him alone.

Recovery of the Land

The Lord is bringing recovery into the land, as well as a beautiful recovery to our personal lives. This is a day of change and a shift for a KINGDOM REVOLUTION. This is our SEASON FOR COMING OUT, and stepping into full recovery and restoration. The Lord is cleansing, purifying and building on a foundation of humility, integrity, and a heart that is surrendered to Him.

We must keep our eyes trained and fixed on our KING. He wants to release us into something so powerful where we can flow by His Spirit.

Isaiah 43:18-19 says, "Do not call to mind the former things, or ponder things of the past. "Behold, I will do something new, Now it will spring forth; Will you not be aware of it? I will even make a roadway in the wilderness, Rivers in the desert."

Once we've walked through the separation with some people, (not being bitter towards them for a wrongdoing in the past but letting it go), then allow God to put us into a new skin, giving us new spiritual sight, a new speech, a new sound, a new song, and new spiritual warfare strategies from Heaven this is what will move us into a new season. THEREFORE get ready, put on your seatbelt, you're about to be catapulted into a Kingdom Revolution.

The following prayer is an awakening prayer. Allow yourself to be opened by the Spirit of God to the new things He is bringing into your life.

Set aside some time to worship the Lord and remove any distractions around you and worship YOUR KING intimately and then say the following prayer. You'll be amazed at what God will do to OPEN THE FOGGY PIPES, if you pray it from your heart. This is an awakening prayer, to set you in a new place. Therefore it's important to take it very serious, and let go of those things that have hindered or lulled you to sleep spiritually.

An Awakening Prayer:

Father God awaken me, awaken my spirit like the dawn of a new day. Fill me with fresh NEW MANNA. Give me new spiritual revelation, and the fresh fire of the Holy Spirit that Joel 2 promises us as a believer. Awaken my eyes that I may see the Glory of the Lord, awaken my ears that I hear the sound of heaven and Father God awaken the voice of a roaring lion in me. We ask YOU LORD as the Lion of Judah to go up before us as we send forth our praise to break the enemy's power over us.

We decree that the Lion of Judah will break the enemy's bow and arrow, as well as his shield, his sword and his weapons of war being used against us in JESUS NAME. Awaken us to Psalms 44:5-7 that says, "Through You we will push back our adversaries; Through Your name, we will trample down those who rise up against us. For I will not trust in my bow, nor will my sword save me. But You have saved us from our adversaries, And You have put to shame those who hate us."

Father God, awaken every dead thing in me, every dead situation in my life, and awaken me from any spiritual apathy, slumber or sleep. Awaken my desire to serve YOU completely, awaken my purpose to fulfill the destiny that YOU HAVE CALLED ME TO, awaken my passion to pursue you with my whole heart. Awaken my feet to walk the path you have for me, awaken my faith to trust you more. Awaken YOUR light IN ME to draw the hopeless to YOU, and awaken the anointing to penetrate the darkness. Awaken righteous indignation to never compromise.

Awaken me to be the Paul Revere who will stand up and sound the alarm to the nations of the world. Awaken me from the disorder of a Babylonian system. Awaken me as a son of God to draw the lost to You. Awaken me to dismantle the enemy in every area of my life. Awaken me to truth and to stand in VICTORY over every area in my life. And awaken me to be an example in my family's life to receive their breakthrough. Awaken Your land, Lord, awaken Your territory Oh God, awaken YOUR churches Oh God, awaken YOUR people Oh God, and awaken YOUR SPIRIT in me. Oh God, awaken me God, Awaken me. In Jesus Name Amen!!!

Part 3

THE PROPHETIC MINISTRY OF SAMUEL

Birthing the True Sons of God in the Earth

When I think of the prophetic, or becoming a Paul Revere; I think of Samuel, who was just a little boy being trained to hear the voice of God. 1 Samuel 3:1-3 says, "Now the boy Samuel was ministering to the LORD before Eli. And the word from the LORD was rare in those days, visions were infrequent. It happened at that time as Eli was lying down in his place (now his eyesight had grown dim and he could not see well), and the lamp of God had not yet gone out."

Much of the church is living on DEAD RELIGION and some of their lamps have gone dim, meaning they are not hearing from God.

As we're going into this new era, God will require us to look for a new strategy. Therefore, we need a sensitivity to know how to move with God and be sensitive to HIS VOICE to arrive where He's taking us.

Transfer of Two Leaderships

Many in the body of Christ are feeling this cross current of two leaderships. In this new era, we will see a transfer of two leaderships flipped. We see this example in Samuel and Eli who represent the **crosscurrent transfer** of two types of leaderships.

THE OLD ORDER of Eli and his sons will be demoted, and the TRUE PROPHETIC who are the Samuel's and the David's (later, whom Samuel anointed) will be promoted to usher in a NEW MOVE OF GOD.

Eli and his sons did not listen to God; therefore, those who are like them are going to be demoted and a new leadership who are like Samuel and David will be promoted.

Eli and his sons were being judged and demoted, (1 Samuel 3:11-18) because they didn't listen to God; they were disobedient to Him, and therefore God will flip a switch in leadership positions that will activate a crosscurrent.

Haven't we already seen that manifested in our government worldview? This confirms what we see in the natural will also transpire in the spiritual realm.

What is a CROSSCURRENT?

What is a crosscurrent? Here are a few definitions: 1) a cross current means running counter to what's trying to come in. 2) a cross current means flowing at an angle to the main current. 3) a cross current means an opposing opinion, influence or a conflicting tendency. 4) a cross current means a conflicting tendency, usually in a plural political sense; it is also an opposing influence.

A cross current will happen between these two types of leadership's that are opposing the move of God. Jealousy will arise from many leaders who will try to control or own it—but they cannot. One group or denomination will not contain this new movement, because ALL THE GLORY BELONGS TO GOD; and it's going to spread like fire around the world. AND GOD WILL NOT ALLOW NO MAN TO TAKE CREDIT FOR IT. (As stated in the beginning of the Book) !!!

The shifting season we're in will include some demotions and some promotions. God is going to raise up the humble, and He is going to demote those who are prideful with wrong motives, and the things that are not of God, they will be demoted. Put it another way, doors are going to open for some, and opportunities will diminish for others. God will move some people unexpectedly because of new assignments that are coming.

Eli and His Sons are a Picture of the DEAD RELIGIOUS WORKS

Eli and his sons are a picture of the DEAD RELIGIOUS WORKS who are out of touch with God. They are fat, comfortable and disrespectful to the new move of God. Eli and his sons were prostituting with the women at the temple doors (1 Samuel 2:22). They were seduced into religious works, as well as promoting themselves, and were more concerned with heaping pleasures upon themselves than they were with pleasing God.

1 Samuel says 2:29- 36 says, 'Why do you kick at My sacrifice and at My offering which I have commanded in My dwelling, and honor your sons above Me, by making yourselves **fat** with the choicest of every offering of My people Israel?' "Therefore the LORD

God of Israel declares, 'I did indeed say that your house and the house of your father should walk before Me forever'; but now the LORD declares, 'Far be it from Me—for those who honor Me I will honor, and those who despise Me will be lightly esteemed. 'Behold, the days are coming when I will break your strength and the strength of your father's house so that there will not be an old man in your house. 'You will see the distress of My dwelling, despite all the good that I do for Israel; and an old man will not be in your house forever. 'Yet I will not cut off every man of yours from My altar so that your eyes will fail from weeping and your soul grieve, and all the increase of your house will die in the prime of life. 'This will be the sign to you which will come concerning your two sons, Hophni and Phinehas: on the same day both of them will die. 'But I will raise up for Myself a faithful priest who will do according to what is in My heart and in My soul; and I will build him an enduring house, and he will walk before My anointed always. 'Everyone who is left in your house will come and bow down to him for a piece of silver or a loaf of bread' and say, "Please assign me to one of the priest's offices so that I may eat a piece of bread."

Yet Samuel positioned himself close to the Ark (God's Word and His Presence) to hear God's voice. Alignment and location will be crucial in hearing God's voice in this new season.

As Samuel stayed in tune with God's voice, he would lay down near the Ark until morning and open the doors of the house of the Lord. One day, Samuel kept hearing God's voice, but he thought Eli the priest was calling him. This was a new position for Samuel, as he was being trained as a Prophet of God.

After three times Eli, the priest realized he was hearing God's voice. 1 Samuel 3:3-9 says, Samuel was lying down in the temple of the LORD where the ark of God was, that the LORD called Samuel; and he said, "Here I am." Then he ran to Eli and said, "Here I am, for you called me." But he said, "I did not call, lie down again." So he went and lay down. The LORD called yet again, "Samuel!" So Samuel arose and went to Eli and said, "Here I am, for you called me." But he answered, "I did not call, my son, lie down again." Now Samuel did not yet know the LORD, nor had the word of the LORD yet been revealed to him. So the LORD called Samuel again for the third time. And he arose and went to Eli and said, "Here I am, for you called me." **Then Eli discerned that the LORD was calling the boy. And Eli said to Samuel, "Go lie down, and it shall be if He calls you, that you shall say, 'Speak, LORD, for Your servant is listening.' "So Samuel went and lay down in his place."**

So Samuel went and laid down and listened for God's voice. 1 Samuel 3:10 says, "Now the LORD came and stood and called as at the other times, "Samuel! Samuel!" And Samuel answered, "Speak, for Your servant is listening."

Samuel's prophetic ear was being trained to hear God's voice as a prophet. Samuel was lying near the ark (God's Word and His Presence) when the Lord commissioned him into his prophetic ministry. Therefore being positioned is very important in this season of promotion.

When Samuel heard THE WORD OF THE LORD, he was afraid to tell Eli the WORD. Then Eli called Samuel and said, "Samuel, my son!" He answered, "Here I am." And he said, "What is the word that the Lord spoke to you? Please do not hide it from me.

God do so to you, and more also, if you hide anything from me of all the things that He said to you." **Then Samuel told him everything and hid nothing from him. And he said, "It is the Lord. Let Him do what seems good to Him**."

Samuel was tested if he would release God's Word to Eli; however he did pass the test. In this new era, we will see God demoting the religious, comfortable sons of Eli and **promoting the obedient sons that have positioned themselves correctly to hear God's voice.**

Listening to God's voice will be a test of every born-again believer, whether your a Prophet or not. I cannot emphasize enough how vital it is we position ourself correctly in regard to how God is leading His people. This hour is so pivotal that God is establishing, and we must stay in tune with the heart of God. In the days ahead of us, elevation will manifest where we will have an opportunity to SHIFT **but we must position our hearts to hear correctly.**

Let me say it again, "In this new era, how we position our heart will be very important." 1 Samuel 3:11-18 says, "The LORD said to Samuel, Then the Lord said to Samuel: "Behold, I will do something in Israel at which **both ears of everyone who hears it will tingle**. In that day **I will perform against Eli** all that I have spoken **concerning his house,** from beginning to end. For I have told him that **I will judge his house forever for the iniquity which he knows, because his sons made themselves vile, and he** (Eli) **did not restrain them. And therefore I have sworn to the house of Eli that the iniquity of Eli's house shall not be atoned for by sacrifice or offering forever."**

Sacred Echoes

God gives us little sacred echoes like he did with Samuel. What is a sacred echo? A repeating statement, like when I heard- "The British are coming" and this powerful Paul Revere message.

We need to pay close attention to the little promptings or sacred echoes we hear from God. Samuel had to learn how to discern the voice of God, by staying close to the Ark (the WORD OF GOD, And PLANTING IT IN OUR HEART).

Samuel is Coming!!

I have GOOD NEWS, Samuel is coming!! Samuel represents the TRUE PROPHETIC that is coming back to the body of Christ. Samuel was coming to anoint David. Samuel 'coming' implies that power, and the true authentic anointing is coming back to the Body of Christ. Samuel 'coming' means divine partnerships, and even miracles are coming.

The true prophetic must partner with God's plan. Remember, everything that Samuel prophesied came to pass because God said, "He would allow **none of his words** to fall to the ground." (1 Samuel 3: 19-21) This means when Samuel spoke, before his words could touch the ground, what he had said would come to pass, because God anointed him.

The Origin of the Anointing

In 1 Samuel 16:1, God sent Samuel to anoint David. What is the Anointing? What does it mean to be anointed? One meaning for the word anointed is 'chosen one.' The New Testament Greek word for 'Anoint' is 'arechiro' and it means to smear or to rub with 'oil' and by implication it means 'to consecrate someone for an office or for a service to God.' Another Greek word, for 'anoint' is 'andaleipho' and again it states 'to anoint with oil to signify God's call on a persons life.'

The origin of anointing was a practice of shepherds to consecrate and set them apart in their commissioned office. Oil in the biblical context refers primarily to olive oil, and not petroleum deposits. Uses of Olive oil was very important for many things such as lighting oil lamps in the temple (Exodus 27:20-21), consecration of the priests, prophets and kings poured oil on their head (Leviticus 8:30), anointing someone for healing as an invocation of God's touch (Leviticus 14:1-18, James 5:14), and even used for some medicinal purposes that fit with the metaphorical usage in anointing for healing.

The origin of anointing was also a practice of shepherds who poured the anointing oil on their sheep's head used for protection (Psalm 23:5). Lice and other insects would often get into the wool of the sheep. Once they moved toward the sheep's head, they would travel into the sheep's ears and kill the sheep. So the ancient shepherds poured oil on the sheep's head to protect them. This made the sheep's wool slippery, making it impossible for insects to get near the sheep's ears because they would slide off. From this we know the anointing brings blessing, protection and empowerment.

The anointing oil is mentioned in God's Word as a metaphor of the Holy Spirit's presence and action in anointing prophets, priests, and kings. For example, when the Prophet Samuel anointed David with oil to be the new king of Israel, the next statement is that "the Spirit of the Lord came mightily upon David from that day forward." (1 Samuel 16:13)

Even the Ram's horn is another metaphor; When Samuel poured the anointing on David's head from a Ram's horn, it not only represented 'David's Kingship' being God's chosen king (1 Samuel 16:13-15), but it also implied power invested in that office.

Jesus is called "The Horn of our Salvation," in Psalms 18 because horns represent dominion and authority given to us to conquer sin and struggles in our life. Therefore 'horns' represent a power that's been entrusted because of our dependency on God. When I was a child, you would hear the old-timers say, "We're going to get a hold of the horns of the altar." The statement represented clinging to God at the altar until you conquered anything that's defeating your life.

Ram's horns were used for fighting, and conquering with invincible strength against opposing enemies. We often miss these significant details; but horns represent something very significant in the scriptures. There were horns on all 4 sides of the Altar of Sacrifice, as well as on the Table of Showbread, and on the Altar of Incense. The horns on the Altar of Sacrifice pointed upward and outward in order to bind the sacrifice to it. The horns on the Altar represent the Lord's kingship, His rule, and His authority over our life. In Psalms 18: 2-3 David said, "The LORD is my rock and my fortress and my deliverer, My God, my rock, in whom I take refuge; My shield and the horn of my salvation, my stronghold. I call upon the LORD, who is worthy to be praised, and I am saved from my enemies." By this we know Adonai, the Lord God was David's king and Lord, whom he served. Yes, David had many weaknesses and shortcomings in his life as well as sin when he committed adultery with Bathsheba, and the murder of her husband, Uriah but he repented and was called a man after God's own heart. (2 Samuel 11, 1 Samuel 13:14, Acts 13:22)

The Lord is going to cause our lives to go higher and stronger than we have ever been before, but we have to be yoked to Him in the battle, and be empowered in the anointing. Therefore, we are being trained and strengthened for our journey, and being developed to overcome.

Transition of Demotion & Promotion

In the book of Isaiah 22:19-25, God speaks about pulling down those appointed to an office that was given by God because they mishandled the anointing. Isaiah 22: 19 says, "I will **depose** you from your office, and I will pull you down from your position."

We must remember when God is setting ONE down, He is setting another ONE up, because He is protecting those who are supposed to be in their NEW positions.

Then in Isaiah 22:20 it says, "Then it will come about in that day, That I will summon My servant **Eliakim** the son of **Hilkiah**."

'Eliakim" means 'God is setting up' and 'Hilkiah' means 'God is protecting'. When we understand God is **setting this up**; and He is **protecting, what**

a peace we can find in knowing that. However everyone that's not in alignment with God's voice will fall. Isaiah 22: 21-22 says, **"I will clothe him** (those that God is promoting) **with your tunic, and tie your sash securely about him** (those that God is demoting), and **I will entrust him with your authority. I will set the key of the house of David on his shoulder and when he opens, no one will shut, and when he shuts no one will open."**

Therefore, we must not promote ourselves. It is the LORD who promotes us, (Psalm 75:6) and it is the LORD who opens doors. If the LORD does not open the door, there is no need to push it open. When people push and promote themselves, it is never the Holy Spirit moving through them; it is always flesh promoting flesh.

As discussed in Chapter 3, the key of David was set on David's shoulder; the place of Apostolic governmental authority. Yes many are feeling the cross current of two leaderships manifesting, however one will be demoted and another will be promoted. God IS SHAPING MANY OF US FOR HIS PURPOSE.

While many Apostolic mentors, both fathers and mothers and prophets, have been prophesying about this cross current transfer, the roar of the LORD IS BEING SOUNDED LIKE NEVER BEFORE. This roar WILL COME as a resounding voice through His people, which means we must have a FEARLESS FAITH. We won't shrink back in the day of battle. We'll be going forward and we'll be running toward the VICTORY because OUR confidence IS IN OUR GOD. This is the voice that's going to shake and paralyze the false authorities at the gate.

Now that we've covered the true prophetic, let's look in the next chapter at what a true apostolic ministry looks like.

Part 4

THE TRUE APOSTOLIC MINISTRY

Birthing the True Sons of God in the Earth

By the time of the New Testament, the word 'apostolos' was already an old word with quite a lengthy history. It carried many shades of meaning — all of which overlapped each other and were interrelated.

When people in the early church heard or read the word "apostle," it is likely they understood an apostle to be a person who was specially selected, commissioned, and sent by the Lord to represent Him for the purposes of the Kingdom: to build up, draw forth, speak out, align, govern, strengthen, and establish His church as His unique agent on the earth.

The Greek word for "apostle" is 'apostolos' which is a compound of the words 'apo' and 'stello'. The preposition 'apo' means 'away' and the word 'stello' means 'to send'. When the two words are combined, they form the word 'apostolos', meaning 'one who is sent away'.

The root of 'apostolos' is the word 'apostello' which appears no less than 131 times in the New Testament and more than 700 times in the Old Testament Greek Septuagint.

At first, it may seem that the definition of this word apostolos — is one who is sent away — denoted one who had been dismissed, set aside, or rejected. However, this word didn't refer to a person sent away in dishonor or disgrace. Rather, the word apostolos was a term of great honor that referred to a person who was selected, commissioned, and sent on an assignment on behalf of a powerful government or individual. Someone did not merely send this person off; he was empowered by God, invested with authority, by a fathering or mothering mentor and then dispatched to accomplish a special task. So, when we talk about apostles, we are discussing individuals who are appointed, empowered, invested with authority by the Lord, and then dispatched to do a special task.

Early believers were also probably aware that the apostle was a pioneer and a chief overseer, responsible for opening new territory, for Kingdom purposes. One who provided passage from one spiritual dimension to another as he took a church to new levels that could never be reached apart from the apostolic anointing.

Yes, believers recognized the apostle as one who had the anointing, authority, and spiritual backing to get things accomplished to further God's purposes. He wasn't just the implementer of pragmatic ideas and strategies. Rather, a true apostle carried within him supernatural insight and revelation that was vital for the growth and the building up of the church. Ephesians 4:11 says, "And He Himself gave some to be apostles".

Many people have taught through denominational teachings, there is no such thing as a living apostle. That all the apostles died at the end of the "Apostolic Age" — along with miracles, signs and wonders, and gifts of the Holy Spirit. That 12 legendary men who walked with Jesus 2,000 years ago, once they died, was the end of that! But over the past decades, we have learned that much of that denominational teaching was wrong.

Some insist that only the original 12 were the ONLY true apostles, but let me give you a concise way of looking at this subject:

In Luke 6:13, Jesus called together His disciples and from among them, He chose 12 men whom He called apostles. They are listed by name in Matthew 10:2-4.

In Luke 9:1-6, Jesus sent forth these 12 apostles to preach the gospel, heal the sick, and cast out demons. But in the next chapter, Jesus appointed 70 more people and "... sent them two by two." (Luke 10:1) When Judas died, Acts 1:25-26 tells us that Matthias was chosen to take his place among the original apostles.

Then we know Paul was also an apostle, who's life testifies of his calling in multiple places throughout the New Testament. Then, thanks to our scholarly ancestors who read and spoke Latin, they converted to calling apostles by the Latin name 'missionaries.' But "missionary" is not a correct term in the context of being an Apostle. Therefore, we are not implying that everyone who is a missionary is an apostle, nor are we saying that there are no missionaries.

Some people are called to be missionaries — these are people who receive a calling to go on a mission to help the work of God. This work is very beneficial and needful, but it does not in itself constitute an apostolic call.

Often these are truly missionaries and not apostles — people who are sent by the local church to help in some way on the mission field. They are very needed in the earth, but that doesn't mean they are an Apostle.

Let's look at the difference in knowing the traits of a true apostle.

Apostles Are Sent Ones

Apostles are sent ones. The word apostle means "a sent one". Sent meaning by the Holy Spirit. This is different from being invited. Sent is different from went. If you're sent, you can't leave. If you are sent to a territory, those in the territory see you there. When you are sent, you can't give up and quit. Apostles are not sent by man, but sent by the Holy Spirit. This is another supernatural aspect of their ministry. In Antioch, the Holy Spirit spoke saying, "Set

Barnabas and Saul apart for Me for the work to which I have called them." (Acts 13:2)

Apostles Are Called by the Lord

An apostolic call originates from a divine revelation and encounter with Jesus Christ. As Paul said, his calling was "... not of men, neither by man, but by Jesus Christ..." (Galatians 1:1)

Therefore apostles are called by the Lord. The Apostle Paul is our example of an apostolic calling. The word 'call' in Greek is 'proskaleomai' meaning a calling of God. (Matthew 10:1). The Scripture says, "Paul, an apostle, not sent from men nor through human agency, but through Jesus Christ and God the Father who raised him from the dead..." (Galatians 1:1).

Notice Paul was called by the Lord Jesus Christ and not by the head of a marketplace or an apostolic network, not a denomination, or even a prophetic presbytery.

Paul had a supernatural encounter with the Lord (Acts 9). This is very different from a heartfelt desire to serve God. This is a profound, supernatural calling, and a function of the Holy Spirit.

Apostles Baptized People in the Holy Spirit

Apostles baptized people in the Holy Spirit with the evidence of speaking in other tongues. You can't be an apostle and ignore the Holy Spirit. Apostle Paul asked, "Did you receive the Holy Spirit when you believed?" And they said to him, "On the contrary, we have not even heard if there is a Holy Spirit." (Acts 19:2)

Unfortunately, there are some so-called apostolic leaders, authors, and network founders that say you can be an apostle without being baptized with the Holy Spirit. Paul thought differently, and the evidence is plain, all New Testament apostles were baptized in the Holy Spirit. Jesus said, "You shall receive power after you are filled with the Holy Spirit" (Acts 1:8). Today we see pastors with no sheep, fishermen called evangelists with no fish, teachers with no students, prophets without purpose, and apostles with no Holy Spirit power. Paul had the same in his day and gave us some counsel in writing saying, "And my speech and my preaching was not with enticing words of man's wisdom, but in demonstration of the Spirit and of power: That your faith should not stand in the wisdom of men, but in the power of God." (1 Corinthians 2:4-5)

Apostles Are Spiritual Fathers/ Mothers

Apostles are spiritual fathers and mothers. They may be apostolic fathers and mothers of the faith, who have spiritual sons and daughters, not just converts, sheep, donors, network members, or television and radio audiences. Real spiritual fathers can be touched, hugged, talked to, and called on the phone.

They will also correct you in love. They are truly concerned about your spiritual condition and your walk with the Lord. True leading fathers and mothers are not always liked. They will correct their spiritual children, lead by example, and bring sons and daughters into maturity. Fathers and mothers will encourage their spiritual children, but they also will cut the flesh with the Word of God.

True fathers and mothers are more interested in building character in their sons and daughters than promoting one's gift or calling. God's Word says, "We can have many instructors but very few fathers." (1 Corinthians 4:14)

In other words, they will tell you the truth because they love and want God's best for you. Apostolic fathers and mothers are easily seen because of their love for people.

Apostles Suffer

Paul defended his apostleship saying "I count all things but loss for the excellency of the knowledge of Christ Jesus my Lord: for whom I have suffered the loss of all things, and do count them but dung, that I may win Christ" (Philippians 3:8) and "That I may know him, and the power of his resurrection, and the fellowship of his sufferings, being made conformable unto his death." (Philippians 3:8-10)

Apostles Are Builders

Apostles are builders. I've seen a few 'apostles' that have never built a birdhouse, much less a ministry. Paul said he was a master builder. 1 Corinthians 3:10 says, "According to the grace of God which was given to me, like a wise **master builder** laid a foundation, and another is building on it. But each person must be careful how he builds on it."

A church is different from a bible study. Two people praying together over at the coffee shop is not a church. A church is not a church until all five-fold ascension gifts are in a spiritual government together to accomplish God's work.

Renting a building to have a meeting is not what Paul was referring to. Inheriting a church that your father built is not what Paul is speaking about. He is using the Greek word 'architektōn' where we get the English word, 'architect.' A true Apostle is described in God's Word as a builder of God's Kingdom.

The Apostle Paul was referred to as an "ascension gift apostle" according to Ephesians 4:8-12. That means his ministry is our best example of a New Testament apostle because he was called after the resurrection and ascension of Christ. The five-fold ascension gift that God called to work with apostles to complete the will of the Lord, which was to establish a governing church where people could be loved, ministered to, and equipped to do what God called them to do.

Yes, restoration of apostles in this generation, void of the humbling training ground of persecution and dying to self, has led to a generation of arrogant, adolescent apostles who feel entitled to the praise of people, who often control others for their own benefit and who consider it a light thing to live carnal lifestyles outside of the pulpit. (This isn't the case with all apostles, but quite a few nonetheless)

More Attention given to gifts than Character

This is not God's fault. This is the result of people giving more attention to the development of their gifts than their character. This is the result of not denying self but using titles and positions to draw attention to oneself, refusing to sacrifice one's reputation for the benefit of the body. This is the result of avoiding persecution through compromise, watering down the truth for personal gain. This is the result of using one's authority to merchandise the anointing and treat people like commodities.

The people in the first century didn't dare join themselves to the apostles or the church itself because of the fear of God. When Ananias and Sapphira lied to the Holy Spirit and fell over dead, that had a way of diminishing the temptation to play church and live selfish lifestyles. When persecution targeted the apostles, that had a way of cutting back on self-promotion into premature apostolic ministries. Business cards with grand apostolic titles were non-existent, and for good reason.

What we've predominantly seen in our day is a mixture of true apostolic ministry blended with religious cultures and carnal lifestyles. But there's change coming. The days are coming upon us when fake titles and immature ministries won't cut it. When dying to self will be a requirement to stand in true apostolic ministry, to withstand severe persecution.

There's a new breed of apostles rising up in the earth who will cling to the cross and they won't flinch with persecution staring them in the face. They don't talk apostolic lingo, they live an apostolic lifestyle. They don't live it up by catering to their flesh. They consider it an honor to suffer shame for His Name. They lay down their lives for their brethren. They don't want people to know they are apostles, they just want people to know Jesus. They pray, love and bless their enemies. They sacrifice their comfort and convenience for the benefit of others. They die so others can live! They sacrifice anything and everything for their sons and daughters. Their hearts are full when their children are successful in their callings, and not when their pockets are full of network dues. This will bring exposure between the real apostles and the wanna be apostles.

Let's Separate the Real Deal from Marketing-Type Apostles

Let's try to separate the real deal from the marketing hype apostles that we see today. In Paul's day, he knew through the power of the Holy Spirit what his call required. There were no limousines, resort hotels, jets, reality televisions programs, or proud millionaire apostles and prophets. Both can have meetings, business cards, conferences, seminars, and prayer lines. Both can get on television, radio, or in a magazine. Both can have a Facebook page, write a book, and organize a great internet website, but when you drill down to the essence of a true apostle you will find valid apostles who are living a very committed life to Christ.

Characteristics of Apostolic Leaders

There is a BIG difference between real apostles and want-to-be apostles. Not everybody is a five-fold ascension ministry apostle. We need apostles, but we need the real deal.

Their godly characteristics are as follows:

- **Called by Jesus Christ Alone**

- **Get people filled with the Holy Spirit**

- **Loving Spiritual Father's and Mother's**

- **Sent Ones**

- **Builders**

Let's Differentiate between Head -Knowledge and Experiential Knowledge

Here we can differentiate between a want-to-be apostle and a real apostle. There are two Greek words that will differentiate the meaning of a true apostle.

They are:

Gnosis=Knowing (From Head knowledge)

Espignosis=Experiential knowledge (From the Spirit)

There's a big difference between head knowledge and experiential knowledge in the Spirit. Want -to be apostles know what they have read or observed, but true apostles have experiential knowledge given by the Spirit of God; seared into every part of their being from paying the price of years and years of submission and dying to self to serve the body of Christ in humility.

Separate True Apostles from Want-to-Be's

To begin, let's see what all apostles can have in common and then separate the true apostle from the want-a-be apostle. Want-to-be apostles don't grieve in their spirits over the condition of the Church because they're more focused on what God has called them to do rather than those who have missed it.

Here's a few characteristic of Apostolic Leaders:

1. They are focused on their assignment. They can't be bought with money or bribed by opportunities to deter them from their assignment.

2. They are concerned with quality, not quantity. They could care less how many people attend their church, how many churches they have under their care or how many leaders look to them for covering. Their desire is to see those

they are in relationship with become everything God called them to be.

3. Their pursuit is to see God's Kingdom expanded, not to build their own kingdom. They don't work to build their own reputation. They just want to see the name of Jesus become famous.

4. They have the heart of the Father. They truly want to see their children far surpass them in their spiritual accomplishments and will do whatever it takes to see that happen. They truly want others to go higher in the blessings of God.

5. They zero in on their jurisdiction, territory, and the people, leaders and churches they have been assigned to assist. They refuse to steal people from other leaders because they respect other leaders and their assignments and jurisdictions. They take seriously those God has given them to develop, oversee, and they don't neglect their responsibility for the sake of personal gain.

6. They don't just talk, they act. They're not about impressing or flattering others. They only speak the truth and they live what they preach.

7. They are full of grace and truth just like Jesus. They have a strong word ministry and function fully in the gifts of the Spirit. Their aim isn't to be a professional orator but to walk in the demonstration of the Spirit, and part of that demonstration is ministering the Word with a spirit of wisdom and revelation that destroys strongholds and sets the captives free.

8. They are very humble and teachable, continuing to learn and develop godly character from the Lord and other leaders. They have a servant's heart and refuse to be idolized by others. They do NOT want to put ANYONE OR THEMSELVES on a pedal stool.

9. They have a divine hatred for the spirit of the world, which tempts them with the lust of the flesh, the lust of the eyes and the pride of life. They refuse to allow carnality to co-exist with the gifts and calling of God. And they don't tolerate these things in leaders they are developing and oversee. They protect the divine investment from the Lord in those they serve.

10. They aren't controlling or demanding. They function in leadership from the perspective of godly influence, and not selfish control.

11. They don't leverage their title or position to take advantage of people for financial gain or other selfish endeavors. This would be unacceptable in the sight of God, and certainly judged by God.

Known Apostles in God's Word

The Apostles we read about in God's Word were sent forth in the New Testament have continued beyond the original 12 apostles, even though many denominations will teach they are non- existent; but that is not true. Apostles are still relevant today.

We can count at least 83 people in the New Testament by name who are called "apostles." We don't have a list of all their names, however, there are 29 listed by name as we know it.

The Scriptures reveal there was a multiplied increase in the apostolic ministry in the Early Church — from 12 to 83 — who were called by God to be apostles.

The following list and scripture references are Apostles found in God's Word:

Jesus Christ (the Chief Apostle)

Paul (Acts 14:14; 22: 21)

Apollos (1 Corinthians 4:6-13)

Eratus (Acts 19: 22)

Tychicus (2 Timothy 4:12)

Epaphroditus (Philippians 2:25; "messenger" is apostolos in the Greek)

James, the Lord's half-brother, convener of Jerusalem Council, author of the Epistle that bears his name (Galatians 1:19; 1 Corinthians 15:7)

Barnabas (Acts 4:36; 14:1, 4,14; 1 Corinthians 9:5,6)

Andronicus (Romans 16:7)

Junia (feminine) (Romans 16:7)

Titus (2 Corinthians 8:23; "messenger" is apostolos in the Greek)

An unnamed brother with Titus (2 Corinthians 8:18,23)

Another unnamed brother with Titus (2 Corinthians 8:22,23)

Timothy (Acts 19: 22; 1 Thessalonians 1:1-4; 2:5-6)

Silas (Silvanus) (Acts 15:23; 1 Thessalonians 1:1-4 & 2:5-6)

Judas (Acts 15: 23; 1 Thessalonians 2:6)

Matthias (Acts 1:26)

Simon Peter (1 Peter 1:1)

Andrew (Peter's brother)

James (Son of Zebedee)

John (James's Brother)

Phillip

Bartholomew/Nathanael

Thomas (also called Didymus)

Matthew/Levi (the Tax Collector)

James (the Son of Alphaeus)

Thaddaeus/Jude (the Son of James)

Simon (the Cananaean/ who was called the Zealot)

Judas Iscariot

Now that we have established what the role of Apostles are let's move forward on what it means to pass the mantle to the next generation.

Part 5

MANTLING THE NEXT GENERATION
Birthing the True Sons of God in the Earth

David like JESUS represents the apostolic mantle being passed to the next generation. Those who are brought into our life; are being passed a mantle to the next generation in many ways.

To understand it's impact is something we pass from past generations that in turn is passed to future generations. This was God's idea to build our floor on their ceiling of those who God plants in our life to take us into higher blessings.

However the only thing that can hinder that is; without giving honor to them there is no impartation. We should always honor those who have gone before us; who imparted and poured into us; because where would we be if they hadn't been there for us? Therefore literally our predecessors are passing a LEGACY to us and in turn we pass it to the next generation as a spiritual inheritance that all eternity will record.

A SONSHIP LEGACY; The Holy and Sure Blessings of David

Like David, we have been designed to serve God's purpose passing a LEGACY to many generations ahead of us. Usually, LEGACY refers to marking GENERATIONS with a godly inheritance. David understood this; he knew about SONSHIP LEGACY CALLED THE HOLY AND SURE BLESSINGS OF DAVID.

Acts 13:32-36 says, "And we preach to you the good news of the promise made to the fathers, that God has fulfilled this promise to our children in that He raised up Jesus. As it is also written in the second Psalm: You are My Son, today I have begotten You. As for the fact that He raised Him up from the dead, no longer to return to decay, He has spoken in this way: 'I will give you the holy and sure blessings of David.' Therefore He also says in another Psalm, 'You will not allow Your Holy One to undergo decay.' "For David, after he had served the purpose of God in his own generation, fell asleep, and was laid among his fathers...."

David is a Typology of Jesus APPOINTING AN APOSTOLIC WARFARE COMPANY who are PROPHETIC

GATEKEEPERS WHO STAND IN THE GAP FOR A KINGDOM MANDATE. When we understand that David, like Jesus is appointing an apostolic warfare company who are prophetic gatekeepers that stand in the gap for a Kingdom Revolution, it can change our perspective on how God's kingdom is set up. In this prophetic hour; this simply means we are partnering with God's end time purpose.

God is going to position gatekeepers in places of authority through Apostolic alignment because it's HIS ORIGINAL BLUEPRINT. God declares in His WORD that the KEY OF DAVID OPENED GATES. Gates represent a place of governmental authority over regions. THEREFORE as a prototype; we recognize this pattern in David's apostolic life.

David stationed prophetic gatekeepers and intercessors in the house of the Lord, to guard against a religious spirit, named Athaliah. She was the daughter of Jezebel. Athaliah represents religion that shuts down the true prophetic. The church is beginning to see new revelation that will come through the new APOSTOLIC WARFARE strategies to stop her.

2 Chronicles 23: 19-21 says, "He (David) stationed the gatekeepers of the house of the LORD, so that no one would enter who was in any way unclean. He took the captains of hundreds, the nobles, the rulers of the people and all the people of the land and brought the king down from the house of the LORD and came through the upper gate to the king's house. And they placed the king upon the royal throne. So all of the people of the land rejoiced and the city was quiet. For they had put Athaliah to death with the sword."

According to 1 Chronicles 9; David appointed all the prophetic gatekeepers in their positions as intercessors. The gatekeepers were positioned at every gate, where there were entrances to the tabernacle on all four sides: east, west, north, and south. They had to guard it, so that no enemy could enter in. They opened the gates morning by morning and stayed all night praying around the house of God. All these who were chosen to be gatekeepers at the thresholds were 212. These were enrolled by genealogy in their villages, whom David and Samuel the seer appointed them in their office of trust. (1 Chronicles 9:22-27)

Athaliah is A Religious Spirit

Athaliah is Jezebel's daughter. When we refer to Jezebel and her seed, we are referring to a religious spirit, and not a real person. The devil wants the church to be fleshy, because he knows that we can't break demonic strongholds operating in the flesh. Jezebel and any of her seed represents religion that tries to control and manipulate man-made systems back into the church.

Our calling is not some sideshow while the really important ministry goes on somewhere else. The Lord has called us and anointed us for greatness. He has poured the resources of His kingdom into us; that we might be counted in a Kingdom Revolution to touch many generations ahead.

The gatekeepers and intercessors had to be alert to Athaliah's tactics and her fleshliness. Athaliah is a Religious Spirit that has to be dealt with ruthlessly. And must be annihilated by the apostolic and prophetic anointing. Therefore God is calling gatekeepers to arise!!! God is calling you and me; He is saying, "Gatekeeper leaders, come forth. May the gift of gatekeeping arise within you for the nations, regions and people. May there be greater realms of authority to equip and empower you through many generations ahead. May we stop being on the defensive and instead engage in an offensive operation in the realm of the Spirit."

"May we take our place of authority in the earth operating as true sons and daughters of God. May we stand at the Ekklesia gates, at the society gates, the media gates, the governmental gates, the educational gates to occupy and establish governmental authority, knowing that the gates of Hell shall not prevail against the Ekklesia."

"May we pluck up, build and plant through the rule and reign of Yeshua. May we follow the Lord; and roar like a lion. Break forth gatekeepers and may you hear the WORD OF OUR GOD to arise and take your place at the GATES!!!"

Psalm 24:7-10 says, "Lift up your heads, O gates, And be lifted up, O ancient doors, that the King of glory may come in! Who is the King of glory? The Lord strong and mighty, The Lord mighty in battle. Lift up your heads, O gates, and lift them up, O ancient doors, that the King of glory may come in! Who is this

King of glory? The Lord of hosts, He is the King of glory. Selah."

Now let's breakdown a better understanding of apostles and prophets in alignment.

Apostles & Prophets in Alignment

True Apostles and Prophets ultimately desire to see a KINGDOM REVOLUTION. Apostles and Prophets need each other. Once they establish a ONENESS together (between apostles and prophets), with true heartfelt alignment it releases a tremendous synergy that blasts through demonic walls and unlocks an unstoppable realm of revelation.

However, many prophets are frustrated because they are trying to relate to an apostolic leader who does not value or understand them. They have tried to submit their gifts to them, but they do not understand how to deal with them, if they aren't relational. Apostles have a unique grace to accept the quirks of prophets and respect their insight, because prophets are strong spiritual warriors. They stand firm in their convictions, and they are unwavering in their revelation and they often have very bold personalities.

There is an EXPLOSIVE SYNERGY THAT IS UNLOCKED WHEN PROPER ALIGNMENT OF THE APOSTOLIC AND THE PROPHETIC COME TOGETHER: AN Example of that would be John the Baptist who was in alignment with Jesus as an Apostle. John the Baptist was a rugged prophetic voice who did not fit into "the box" of ministry in that day. He carried a wilderness cry to prepare people for the coming of the Lord.

What is a Mantle?

Many of you may be wondering what a mantle is. A mantle in the old covenant was a loose outer garment that the prophet wore. Their mantle represented an office that came with an authority and the supernatural power of God that was released through their mentor to function in that office.

We read about how God called Elisha to link up with Elijah, and immediately Elisha left the oxen and ran after Elijah. From this example; we see if we want to get what the previous generation had, we have to be under their training and spend time serving them in some capacity faithfully. (1 Kings 19:20)

Elisha asked for a double portion of Elijah's anointing and Elijah's response was "If you see me when I go up, you shall surely receive it." And truly Elisha caught the mantle when Elijah went up and did double miracles.

ELIJAH-ELISHA MENTORING

Elijah mentored Elisha to prepare him in his ministry, and Elisha stayed with him, until one day God took Elijah up by a chariot of fire to heaven. Elisha did indeed stay at his post of training; when he saw Elijah taken up in a chariot of fire, (some call it a whirlwind) Elijah's mantle fell to the ground, and Elisha picked it up and tested the mantle to be sure it was activated in his life, and this was a sign to Elisha that the God of Elijah was with him.

God gave Elijah clear instructions to cast his mantle on Elisha (the next generation) and when he did, there was a huge shift in his ministry. Elisha received a double portion of Elijah's anointing and did double the miracles than Elijah. For example, part of the supernatural manifestation that came through the mantle that God gave to Elijah was he performed many miracles such as raising the dead, multiplying oil with the widow woman, and healing the sick, and many more.

We need ELIJAH-ELISHA mentoring who will pass a mantle to the next generation in order to see a KINGDOM REVOLUTION MOVEMENT. True apostolic fathers/ mothers establish, equip and release the next generation into their ministry like Elijah and Elisha.

Truly we need to see the Elijah's come forth to father/ mother the Elisha's for the next generation because it will take an apostolic strength and stability to mantle the next generation.

God is releasing mantles on those who served Him and departed from the earth; and now the mantles are coming down to those who are connected to them spiritually.

In 2 Kings 3, after Elijah had poured into Elisha; it is very evident the spiritual pipes opened up that were previously blocked, and the atmosphere completely shifted. The hindrance in Elisha's case came from his surroundings. He was in a camp of people where three nations mixed their discordant beliefs and needless to say there was no water, and the men-at-arms were slowly perishing.

Three kings had waited on the prophet; and the confusion and clamour must have been great. What memories were awakened in the mind of Elisha as he acted rightly, and bravely remembering how Elijah had trained him. When he saw Jehoram coming to him for help, he challenged him saying --"What business do you have with me? What have I to do with you? Go to your father's prophet's and your mother's prophets." But the king of Israel said to him, "No, for the Lord has called these three kings together to hand them over to Moab."

Elisha said, "As surely as the Lord of armies lives, before whom I stand, if I did not respect Jehoshaphat the king of Judah, I would not look at you nor see you. **But now bring me a minstrel**."

What does BRING ME A MINSTREL imply?

When Elisha said; "Bring me a minstrel" in 2 Kings 3:15, this represents teaching the next generation what true worship is. As the true Elijah's come forth to teach and train the Elisha's of this next generation, we will see mantles released to the next generation because it's a matter of life and death.

A PIVOTAL SHIFT

Understanding this kingdom principle will bring us into a pivotal shift. This was a PIVOTAL SHIFT that came about, when the minstrel played, that the hand of the Lord came upon Elisha. In 2 Kings 3, we read the passage where the Kings of Israel, Judah and Edom were in pursuit of the Moabites and they went into the desert and realized that they were completely out of water. There was no water for them or their horses, which represents a spiritual drought.

Wisely, they asked for a prophet to come on the scene! Elisha came and saw they were in dire straits. He looked at their situation and then said, "**Bring me a minstrel!**" (v. 15). While the minstrel (harpist) began to play; the hand of the Lord came upon Elisha and then he prophesied this:

2 Kings 3:16-17a says, And he (Elisha) said, "This is what the Lord says, 'Make this valley full of trenches. For the Lord says this: 'You will not see wind, nor will you see rain, yet that valley shall be filled with water, so that you will drink, you and your livestock, and your other animals. And this is a significant thing in the sight of the Lord; He will also give the Moabites into your hand. And it happened in the morning about the time of the offering of the sacrifice, that behold,

water came from the direction of Edom, and the country was filled with water."

Wow! You may need to go back and read this again! Elisha, because of the anointing upon the worship, he prophesied the WORD OF THE LORD that they were to start digging ditches because God was about to send water! If you read on, you'll find out that an **awesome miracle manifested.** As Elisha prophesied the Word of the Lord; water filled the trenches everywhere. And God gave them complete victory over the Moabites!

Teaching the Next Generation About True Worship

This generation has been caught up in entertainment instead of true worship. It has been my concern for a very long time that the worship of this present generation is often just simple entertainment.

We must teach them about true worship and an intimate adoration expressed to the Lord rather than religious performance. Therefore we must realize the power of worship that releases an anointing to prophesy the Word of the Lord, and it releases direction and will **manifest miracles.** Amazing, right? So, the mantles on the Elishas will empower them to move even more boldly during worship to declare the WORD of the Lord.

We need to become true worshipers and be determined to be a part of the upcoming Elijah-Elisha Revolution! This would bring a KINGDOM REVOLUTION FOR SURE IN THE EARTH AND THATS WHAT GOD LONGS FOR IN THE TRUE SONS OF GOD!!!

Prayer: Lord, Let the Fathers arise, and let the sons and daughters arise to bring glory through true authentic worship to OUR KING AS WE SHIFT INTO A KINGDOM REVOLUTION for such a time as this!!!

Present Day Elijah's

God is setting His present-day Elijah's in the earth, and He is calling us to confront the false prophetic, but it will only manifest through true worship to Jehovah. God is pulling down Ahab and Jezebel from their high places, and I believe we are about to see a GREAT DEMONSTRATION OF GOD'S POWER in the earth realm.

This is the hour that changes the world, and the Lord is giving us a front row seat to the greatest display of HIS SOVEREIGNTY the earth has ever seen. We need to get ready for this great season of planting and watering because it's going to bring a great harvest. The earth is groaning to see the TRUE Sons of God manifested. There needs to be an overthrow of evil and corruption, so that GOD'S KINGDOM can be established. The church needs to be become like Paul Revere, willing to expose the spiritual darkness and participate with heaven's plan.

As leader's, the Elijah generation has the responsibility to nurture the Elisha generation and protect them from wolves, dogs, goats, foxes, false prophets, evil workers, and the evil deceivers. (Matthew 7:15; Acts 20:29; Philippians 3:2; Matthew 25:32; 2 Timothy 4:14)

Yes, God is the judge and only He can make the final decision of one's' salvation. However to negate all life-giving correction by saying God is the judge does a disservice to the very ones that need to hear the scriptural truth.

Again, to judge means to render a decision, form an opinion, or to decide where's there's scriptural error. Therefore, identifying scriptural error means that we are supposed to "try the spirits" and know them by their fruit. Next time someone tells you not to "test the spirits" remember this scripture. 1 John 4 1-2 says, "Beloved, do not believe every spirit, but test the spirits to see whether they are from God, because many false prophets have gone out into the world. By this you know the Spirit of God..."

We aren't called to judge people's sins, but we are told to "test the spirits" and "know them by their fruit." There is the Holy Spirit, human spirits, and demonic spirits. We must discern the difference as believers.

According to the Thayer Greek Lexicon, "try" is the Greek word 'dokimazo' and it means:

- To test, examine, prove, and scrutinize.
- To see whether a thing is genuine or not.
- To recognize as genuine after examination, to approve, and deem worthy.

Therefore spirits are judged according to what they say and how they act through people.

According to Jesus, the only way to know what's inside a person is to know them by their fruit. Matthew 7:15-20 says, "**Beware** of the false prophets, who come to you in sheep's clothing, but inwardly are ravenous wolves. You will know them by their fruit. Grapes are not gathered from thorn bushes, nor figs from thistles, are they? So every good tree bears good fruit, but the bad tree bears bad fruit. A good tree cannot bear bad fruit, nor can a bad tree bear good fruit. Every tree that does not bear good fruit is cut down and thrown into the fire. So then, you will know them by their fruits."

Jesus used this example on how to know a tree by its fruit.

Matthew 7:15 says, "**Beware** of the false prophets, who come to you in sheep's clothing, but inwardly are ravenous wolves", therefore we must be discerning more than ever. Therefore, our measurement for the truth is the written Word of God.

The word "**beware**" in Matthew 7 which means to use extreme caution because some are wolves in sheep's clothing who have come to devour the sheep.

Stay or Leave the Church

Some ask if they should stay in a church when the leadership has a Jezebel spirit. Let's ask some practical questions.

- Why should someone stay?

- Why should someone leave?

- What would be the result if you left and a family member stayed? Sometimes it takes confrontation to get free.

Anywhere that you can see manipulation and control being exercised through the leadership within the government, society, the church, or the home means there is a Jezebel there. Staying in a church with Jezebel leadership is a spiritual death sentence. Life is too short to put up with spiritual abuse.

If you're in a church controlled by the Jezebel spirit, get out now and don't look back. The scripture says, "But examine everything carefully; hold fast to that which is good; abstain from every form of evil." (1 Thessalonians 5:21-22)

We must be forewarned when looking at the life of Elijah, when he challenged the 450 Prophets of Baal, the Apostolic mantle on him caused a demonic stirring, exposed the darkness, and tore down their false idols. We know that in the story of Elijah and the prophets of Baal and Asherah, Elijah devised a plan to set up altars where the gods of Baal and Asherah could show their power and then an altar was prepared where the one true God would show His power. Elijah then sets the standard by declaring, "...The God who answers by fire--He is God."

How Long Will You Waver between Two Opinions

1 Kings 18:21 says, "How long will you waver between two opinions?" This was at a crucial time in Israel where the false had to be revealed to see what God you were going to serve. We know that Elijah went before all Israel and offered this verbal challenge, saying, "If the Lord is God, follow Him; but if Baal is God, follow him." (I Kings. 18:21b)

As I meditated on this scripture one day, I felt like God showed me that Elijah's question is still relevant for many of us today. We can find ourselves wavering between two opinions, between what is true and what is false.

Elijah, the prophet was calling the hearts of the people to quit being wishy-washy and decide once and for all whether they will follow God or Baal. Elijah confronted the prophets of Baal and Asherah on Mount Carmel to see who their GOD would be.

It's no different TODAY, as believers; we must take a stand and declare who will be OUR GOD. We must come out from among them in the world, come out of a place of wavering and into a greater depth of commitment and standing out from the world.

It is no surprise that the prophets of Baal and Asherah failed miserably because no god came to consume their sacrifice. Elijah gives the orders to prepare the altar for God to come with fire and He is so sure of His coming that he gives the command to soak the altar with water three times. And then, the God of glory answered with His fire! God's fire consumed everything on the altar even licking up the water in the trenches. Through this demonstration, the hearts of the people turned, and they left their false god wavering behind. 1 Kings 18: 39 says,

"When all the people saw this, they fell prostrate and cried, "The LORD--he is God! The LORD he is God!"

Like, Elijah, we must learn how to differentiate between the enemy's voice and God's voice. We must turn down all the distractions and the voices of Babylonian contradiction.

Our ONLY solid foundation must be built on God's Word, and nothing else. That's the only foundation that isn't faulty but is totally reliable because it's built on an unshakable kingdom. Isaiah 7:9 says, "If you don't stand firm in your faith, you won't stand at all."

We often don't see our independence and self-reliance where we are self-willed. We don't even realize where we have set up our independence on the world's way of doing things, instead of following God's way. God has to reveal it to us, by making it come to the surface, through circumstances and through our relationships.

We often think worldliness is living corrupt. But really worldliness is rooted in man's own independence. When we listen to the wrong influences it can cause us to lose our passion and then it spreads into our soul to delude the truth that we know.

There is nothing wrong with processing things and thinking things through, but anytime there is double-mindedness we will feel the confusion because its coming through our intellect instead of our spirit man.

Israel's problem was not totally rejecting God. Their problem was they wanted to worship God and Baal. God calls that a divided allegiance or a deluded mixture. And that is what we must stand firmly against!

We can't afford to vacillate between two opinions. The word 'vacillate' comes from the word 'Vaseline.' We don't need to slip and slide everywhere because it's not wise. James 1:6-8 (NASB) says, "But he must ask in faith without any doubting, for the one who doubts is like the surf of the sea, driven and tossed by the wind. For that man ought not to expect that he will receive anything from the Lord, being a double-minded man, unstable in all his ways."

The Greek word for being 'double minded' is 'dipsuchos' in James 1:8, in its literal translation it means 'double-souled,' like having two independent wills. Double-mindedness is literally having two separate minds holding contradictory thoughts. A double-minded person is restless and unstable in all their ways. They're confused in their thoughts, actions, and behavior. Such a person is always in conflict with themselves. This is serious because a broken focus will destroy your destiny.

James 1:7-8 says, "For that man ought not to expect that he will receive anything from the Lord, being a double-minded man, unstable in all his ways." Therefore whatever has the capacity to hold your attention has power over you!!!

Therefore be intentional; Tell God your need for Him and thank Him for all He has done. Proverbs 3:5-6 says, "Trust in the Lord with all your heart and lean not onto your own understanding. In all your ways acknowledge Him, And He will make your paths straight."

The Voices of Babylon

The voices of Babylon are getting louder and louder. We must make a conscious effort not to allow the voices of Babylon to be heard louder than the voice of God, thereby exercising discernment to know the difference between the two.

The Lord wants us to hear His voice but if we're listening to too many other voices—we will be confused. One way to tell the difference is Babylon voices will always have selfish motives, saying, "What is in it for me?" Many will not hear God's voice because they have been deafened through listening to the voices of other people's opinion that speak in the interests of self.

There is coming a rising crescendo of the voices of Babylon that are going to try to deafen our ears to God's still small voice, but we've got to decide, "Who's voice are we going to listen to?"

The Lord is calling us to arise from the place of slumber sleep, and we must not allow the voice of the enemy to be louder than God's voice.

Let me say it AGAIN; God's voice always speaks in the interests of HIS KINGDOM, but the voices of Babylon will always speak in the interests of self. And that's how you discern the difference between the two.

These are dangerous times to be unaware. We must learn how to turn down the distractions of the world. God longs to bring us from the noise of men that clamor for our attention to abide in the secret place with Him.

Originated in the Tree of the Knowledge of Good and Evil

The Babylonian voices that are getting louder and louder are the SAME VOICE that originated in the tree of the knowledge of good and evil when Adam and Eve were in the garden. It still resonates a sound through everything that is of the earth. James says it's sensual, earthly and it's demonic.

James 3: 6-18 says, "How great a forest is set ablaze by such a small fire through their tongue! The tongue is a fire, a world of iniquity. The tongue is set among our members, staining the whole body, setting on fire the entire course of their life, and set on fire by hell. There is no human being who can tame the tongue. It is a restless evil, full of deadly poison. With it we bless our Lord and Father, and with it we curse people who are made in the likeness of God. From the same mouth comes blessing and cursing. My brothers, these things ought not to be so. Does a spring pour forth from the same opening both fresh and salt water? Can a fig tree, my brothers, bear olives, or a grapevine produce figs? Neither can a salt pond yield fresh water. We need wisdom from above. But if you have bitter jealousy and selfish ambition in your hearts, do not boast and be false to the truth. This is not the wisdom that comes down from above, but is earthly, unspiritual, and demonic."

"For where jealousy and selfish ambition exist, there will be disorder and every vile practice. But the wisdom from above is first pure, then peaceable, gentle, open to reason, full of mercy and good fruits, impartial and sincere. And yields to a harvest of righteousness that is sown in peace by those who make peace."

The Apostolic Anointing brings Jezebel down through Prayer

This is the time that the Lord is calling us to put on our combat boots on and engage in battle through intercession. Many will begin to see new revelation that will come through apostolic warfare strategies because the warfare has intensified. Matthew 11:12 says, "...the kingdom of Heaven suffers violence, and the violent take it by force." Now is the time to arise intercessors and shake off complacency, fear or any other thing holding you back.

This is not the time for God's people to retreat and run and hide in a cave. How did Elijah go from 'God's man of faith and power for the hour who challenged 450 Baal prophets, to now a prophet of God running and hiding in a cave? What happened? Well we forget that he was a man just like us. (James 5:17) One day he is outrunning a horse-driven chariot and the next day he's trying to outrun Jezebel. One day he's calling fire out of heaven and another he sets on a blazing run into the desert as a coward.

In 1 Kings 19:4, Elijah was exhausted, experiencing depression, he was vulnerable, and instead of fighting, he ran. He had had enough - and was ready to check out.

There are times that 'depression' may just be a medical condition requiring treatment at some level, but there are also times that spiritual depression is linked to an attack of 'witchcraft.' Witchcraft is insidious. It seeks to control and destroy your life. It seeks to find your vulnerabilities and then move in for the kill shot.

The 'key' for Elijah to come out of the cave and stop having the suicidal thoughts was for him to 'hear' the voice of God. When God called him out of the cave and to stand on the mountain in His presence, He was being trained on how to hear God's voice, and how to resist the enemy's voice. The scripture says, God's voice was NOT in the wind —God's voice was NOT in the earthquake —God's voice was NOT in the fire. No, God's voice wasn't in none of them. God's voice came in the gentle whisper.

As we learn to wrap our face in the mantle God has released to us; God's voice will be heard when we turn away from the earth quake, the fire and the wind representing different elements of circumstances we go through.

When God told Elijah to come out of the cave and to stand on the mountain in His presence, He tested Elijah on how to hear the true from the false. God was training him to know the difference. The enemy was trying to use these elements to distract Elijah, but Elijah didn't listen to them; he got down in a birthing position of intercession and this is how he received a breakthrough.

The Lord wants His people to ARISE and come out of the cave and position ourselves in a birthing position of prayer, like Elijah did.

Let's establish AGAIN SOME TRUTHS ALREADY WRITTEN ABOUT ELIJAH, but for the purpose of reiterating some principles in our own life.

• Elijah was a man of prayer and intercession.

• Elijah brought fire down from heaven, but he also prayed for rain during a drought and it rained.

• Elijah received a breakthrough when he positioned himself in a birthing position of intercession. (I Kings 19:13)

THIS IS A VERY IMPORTANT NOTICE: Spirit of Witchcraft is a Territorial/ Principality in the Second Heaven

There is a level of spiritual warfare we must be warned about. On this level of spiritual warfare, principalities and powers are dealt with through corporate intercession for a region, under apostolic authority. Elijah ran into a territorial spirit, in the second heaven called the Spirit of Witchcraft, who came under the spell of Jezebel. A territorial spirit cannot be cast out of people, nor are we supposed to do warfare against principalities alone or with small groups. This can cause all kinds of warfare that alone you're NOT equipped to handle. Be forewarned; you don't want needless casualties of war.

Principalities do not dwell in people; they dwell in heavenly places (a ruler in the second heaven) and can ONLY BE DISPLACED through corporate apostolic unity of warfare.

Once again to clarify; the Spirit of Witchcraft is a principality or a ruler in the second heaven. The Spirit of Witchcraft (in the second heaven) is different from a witchcraft spirit (on ground level warfare who can dwell in people).

As believers we have ground level authority to come against a witchcraft spirit, but NOT the principalities of witchcraft in regions by ourselves. This is very dangerous and catastrophic.

Elijah was given apostolic authority in this realm of spiritual authority because God gave him that region (jurisdiction) to move in the supernatural to declare the Word of the Lord. The word 'jurisdiction' means the official power to make legal decisions and judgments.

As an APOSTOLIC OFFICE THATS BEEN GIVEN A JURISDICTION BY GOD, now we can understand why it takes corporate warfare to displace principalities and spiritual wickedness in high places. However doing spiritual warfare alone or with small groups is a death sentence. Please don't do that!!

Jezebel releases the FALSE PROPHETIC

We must understand that Jezebel releases THE FALSE prophetic. And in this hour that we're standing in, we must discern between the two.

Therefore the Apostolic brings in the strategy to bring Jezebel (Principality) down corporately and remove false authorities at the gate to see them taken back for God. This qualifies protection when you follow Apostolic protocol, because of their legal jurisdiction with God.

Church leaders and the Church have left this spirit alone for the sake of peace and fearing the consequences of what Jezebel will do. Remember when Jehu arrived to take down Jezebel, she asked him, "Is it peace Zimri?" (2 Kings 9:31)

Jezebel wanted Jehu to make peace with her. Jehu did the right thing and was NOT going to tolerate this spirit operating in Israel any longer because this was his jurisdiction given to him by God.

Therefore, Jehu said to the eunuchs, "Throw her down." Then they threw Jezebel to the ground where Jehu's horse trampled her under his hooves. And the dogs licked up her blood.

The Lord said this about Jezebel in Revelations 2:18-23, "And to the angel of the church in Thyatira write: The Son of God, who has eyes like a flame of fire, and His feet are like burnished bronze, says this: 'I know your deeds, and your love and faith and service and perseverance, and that your deeds of late are greater than at first.' 'But I have this against you, that you tolerate the woman Jezebel, who calls herself a prophetess, and she teaches and leads My bond-servants astray so that they commit acts of immorality and eat things sacrificed to idols.' **'I gave her time to repent,** and she does not want to repent of her immorality.'

God is merciful but if we continue to rebel against His authority, this is what He says He will do to Jezebel: 'Behold, I will throw her on a bed of sickness, and those who commit adultery with her into great tribulation, unless they repent of her deeds. 'And I will kill her children with pestilence, and all the churches will know that I am He who searches the minds and hearts; and I will give to each one of you according to your deeds.'

A Revolutionary Shift

Therefore to displace Ahab and Jezebel mentalities, there must be a revolutionary shift in minds and hearts. The Jezebel and Ahab mentalities that facilitate the high places are being exposed. The Lord is positioning many to get in their God ordained places.

Therefore we see through Jezebel's evil intentions; she uses intimidation and rejection against the TRUE apostolic and prophetic gifts. Let's explain deeper.

When Jezebel married King Ahab of Israel; she persuaded him to introduce the worship of the Tyrian god Baal-Melkart, a nature God that **despised God's prophets. Most of the prophets of Yahweh were**

killed at her command. You can read it in the scriptures. By that evidence we understand she opposes the true prophetic.

God will not tolerate this and it must be addressed. Yet we can be sure of this; God is going to expose the true prophetic from the false prophetic. The Holy Spirit is putting a **laser beam** on it in this hour exposing it for true kingdom freedom to manifest.

This will require a **revolutionary shift** as we enter realms of heavenly warfare as an apostolic team that comes through unity and intercession together to demonstrate a KINGDOM REVOLUTION.

This is why we must stay in corporate unity. We must not lose our focus as an Apostolic Team; as this is a strategic time where God is displacing the strategy of hell that has contaminated His people through Jezebel and Ahab mentalities through regions, and even in our government.

There is a way out but first we must recognize their tactics. Also please understand a Jezebel spirit is not limited to a female gender ONLY. We've seen in many cases it can operate in a man or a woman; because it's a spirit.

Therefore don't lock yourself into a mindset that a Jezebel is a female gender only; because nothing could be further from the truth.

We will recognize these personality traits of Jezebel on the following chart:

Criticism	Ungrateful	Gossip/ Slander	Rejection of Truth	Many forms of abuse
Ignores People	Clairvoyant	Sexual Perversion	Twisted Pride	Preoccupati on with self
Attempts to make you look like you're the Jezebel	Presumption/ Independent	Possessive Love (turns from sweet to sour if they don't	Pushiness/ Commands Attention	Vindictivene ss
Uses people to accomplish	Insubordinati on/Rebellion	Excessive Bragging & Talking	Persuasive	Pushy & Domineerin g
Sowing seeds of discord	Need to accomplish her/ his will (at anyone's	Sequesters- Information	Religious/ Spiritualizes everything	Volunteers for everything
Hate	Know it all	Gift Giving to buy love	Insinuates Disapproval	Takes credit for everything

Intimidation, Vengeful & Spiteful	One-man team	Ambitious	Uses the Element of Surprise	Lies
Low Self-esteem	Distortion	With holds & Uses Information	Refuses to admit guilt or wrong	Talks in confusion

Jezebel operates in haughtiness, fear, whoredom, lying, perverseness, error, jealousy, and bondage. She uses loneliness, deception, discouragement, confusion, depression, sexual perversion, enticement, rejection, disorientation, and withdrawal, feelings of worthlessness, despair, defeat, and even suicide.

She had many evil personality traits, but she was given an opportunity to repent.

If God is revealing a need for repentance of the Jezebel personality in your life, say the following prayer. He will forgive you, when you mean it from your heart.

Prayer of Repentance from a Jezebel personality: Father God, I acknowledge that if I have yielded myself to the personality of Jezebel, I ask You to forgive me. Please forgive me for every time that I have opened myself to the Jezebel personality; to control and manipulate others.

Through the power of the Holy Spirit, I pull down this stronghold and I command all spirits of haughtiness, fear, insecurity, whoredom, lying, perverseness, error, jealousy, and bondage to leave me in the Name of Jesus. Please open my eyes where Jezebel tendencies have operated in my life; expose it to me, and transform me. In Jesus mighty Name, I claim Your Lordship over my life.

Part 6

THE GREAT CROSSOVER

Birthing the True Sons of God in the Earth

What does it mean to be a 'HEBREW'? To be acknowledged as a 'HEBREW' means 'YOU'VE CROSSED OVER.' The word 'HEBREW' in its simplest definition means 'one from beyond who has crossed over'.

Essentially, we all have to decide to crossover as a SPIRITUAL HEBREW if we're born again. To be a Hebrew is a person who has crossed over from death to life; from a life of sin to a life of righteousness but it goes much deeper than that; When you've crossed over spiritually; you're truly walking in your identity as a true son of God in Christ with a KINGDOM REVOLUTION MANDATE.

You're no longer a SLAVE TO SIN or in bondage to obeying false gods of this Babylonian system; but now you've been transformed into SONSHIP. We've been called out of darkness into His marvelous light: (1 Peter 2:9). We're a people who have crossed over from a life of slavery into a life of freedom and victory as a true son of God.

Abram was the first person to be called a Hebrew, even though he was from Ur of the Chaldean's who served other gods. (Genesis 11:31) Abraham crossed over as it's confirmed many times. Joshua 24:2-3 says, Joshua said to all the people, "This is what the Lord, the God of Israel says: 'From ancient times your fathers lived beyond the Euphrates River, namely, Terah, the father of Abraham and the father of Nahor, and **they served other gods**. Then I took **your father Abraham** from **beyond** the Euphrates River and led him through all the land of Canaan, and multiplied his descendants and gave him Isaac."

In the above passage we see a distinction between Abram before he crossed over to the life he was called to live after he crossed over. Abram served other gods beyond the river, but when he crossed over, he was TOTALLY DIFFERENT. This characteristic of 'crossing over' becomes part of the Hebrew experience, and is seen as part of the journey of all of God's people.

This makes sense, as the first time we see the word 'Hebrew' used is when Abram is called 'Abram the Hebrew' in Genesis 14:13, in God's Word.

Genesis 14:13 says, "Then a survivor came and told Abram the Hebrew..." It should be noted that the story of Abraham who is "the father of many nations" is connected to the word "Abar" which also means to cross-over, as we see it is one of the first things mentioned about him. Genesis 17: 5 says, "No longer shall you be named Abram, but your name shall be Abraham; For I have made you the father of a multitude of nations."

So it is now abundantly clear why Abram was called a Hebrew. Genesis 12:4-6 says, "So Abram went away as the Lord had spoken to him; and Lot went with him. Now Abram was seventy-five years old when he departed from Haran. Abram took his wife Sarai and his nephew Lot, and all their possessions which they had accumulated, and the people which they had acquired in Haran, and they set out for the land of Canaan; so they came to the land of Canaan."

This repeats again and again with Israel as they crossed the Red Sea into freedom. When God spoke to Moses about the Passover sacrifice, He Himself said that when the death Angel saw the blood, He would 'pass over' or 'cross over' using the same word

'Abar' (H5674 – עבר – 'âbar) and interchangeably with 'Ivri' (H5680– עִבְרִי – ivri) means 'to pass over'.

Exodus 12:12 (NASB) says, "For I will **go through** the land of Egypt on that night, and fatally strike all the firstborn in the land of Egypt, from the human firstborn to animals; and against all the gods of Egypt I will execute judgments—I am the Lord."

And Exodus 12:23 says, "For the Lord will **pass through** to strike the Egyptians; but when He sees the blood on the lintel and on the two doorposts, the Lord will **pass over** the door and will not allow the destroyer to come in to your houses to strike you."

In Exodus 15, they sang the Song of Moses, after they crossed over the Red Sea. Exodus 15:16 -18 says, "Terror and dread fall upon them; by the greatness of Your arm they are motionless as stone, Until Your people **pass over**, Lord, Until the people pass over whom You have purchased. You will bring them and plant them in the mountain of Your inheritance, the place, Lord, which You have made as Your dwelling, The sanctuary, Lord, which Your hands have established. The Lord shall reign forever and ever."

Therefore we see crossing over was a distinct feature of God's chosen people who identified themselves as Hebrews both in the Old and the New Testament.

Like the patriarchs, we should never forget the most important characteristic of being a spiritual Hebrew; where there is a willingness to cross over in Covenant with the Lord as a believer in Christ who is brought into the promise land. As we live fully surrendered to the Father, He is guiding us every step of the way, establishing us in His Kingdom plans. Crossing over really boils down to our total surrender by SIMPLE OBEDIENCE.

The power source of JESUS' LIFE was connected to HIS RADICAL OBEDIENCE TO THE FATHER. Jesus said in John 4: 34, "My food is to do the will of Him who sent Me, and to finish His work."

Therefore there is a great grace, authority and power in our total surrender. There will be unexpected twists and turns; unseen detours may pop up, but it is all part of the journey! Proverbs 3:5-6 says, "Therefore trust in the Lord with all your heart, and lean not on your own understanding; in all your ways acknowledge Him, and He will direct your paths."

A Vision of a Great Crossover

I'm going to move now into a vision God gave to me many years ago. I was walking across a very narrow bridge following Jesus. At the first glimpse, it looked like a tightrope. But as the Lord gave me a closer look where I saw a very narrow bridge that I was crossing over to the other side of a steep jagged deep canyon. Then the Lord said to me, "Let's cross over to the other side!" As I looked down, I froze in fear because the canyon was so deep and jagged, and the bridge was moving with ropes on the handrails. But as long as I crossed over keeping my eyes on Jesus, I could move forward. The Lord was taking me across the bridge toward a beautiful bright light beyond the canyon. Then I saw other people trying to cross over, but they were carrying heavy baggage and some looked like they were dressed as executives and some were dressed in casual clothes. However they were not allowed to crossover into the glorious light until they left their baggage behind. The Lord showed me their baggage represented self–promotion. I ask the Lord what this meant. And He said, "No one can crossover with their baggage into My Third Day glory, and there can be no trace of self-promotion."

What I saw "in the spirit" was everyone had to leave their baggage behind. The bridge in the vision that everyone crossed over was so very narrow, that it would not allow any baggage to be carried on it. Therefore, they had to decide to let go of their baggage in order to cross over to the other side.

Saul Hid Behind His Baggage

Then one day, shortly after this vision, the Lord had me studying 1 Samuel 9-10. Samuel had arrived to anoint Saul as king, when the people inquired for Saul; and it says, they found him hiding himself **behind the baggage.** 1 Samuel 10:22 says, "Therefore they inquired further of the LORD, "Has the man (Saul) come here yet?" So the LORD said, **"Behold, he is hiding himself by the baggage**."

When Samuel arrived to anoint Saul, we read that Saul had been on a search for his father's donkeys. (Samuel 9:1-6) 1 Samuel 9:20, says, "As Samuel arrived to anoint Saul, they told Saul, "As for your **father's donkeys** which were lost three days ago, **do not set your mind** on them, for they have been found." The donkeys that Saul went to look for known as **'his father's donkey's'** are a representation of '**our flesh nature**' and searching for things that fulfill the carnal appetite known as '**our lower flesh nature**'.

We often hide behind our baggage just like Saul did; and this is the baggage that we must let go of that I saw in my vision. Baggage represents bondages to strongholds that we've yielded our flesh nature to.

In my vision of crossing over; none could crossover until they let go of their baggage. Baggage can be so many things: like lust in many forms, compromise, religion, and works of the flesh, fear, alcohol, addictions and many other strongholds; even things like passivity and a lack of passion for the things of God, or even anger, and unforgiveness.

The Third Day Glory who Graduate as Kings

In my vision, the Lord showed me, this crossing over is a picture of the Third Day Church being set apart for God's purpose. The Lord reinforced saying to me, "Everyone who crossed over must leave their present day baggage if they want to cross over to the other side to enter the things that I've prepared for My people." Then I saw in the vision; the Lord placed crowns on their heads 'AS KINGS' when they let go of their baggage, they were given keys in their place of authority. These crowns and keys represent ruling and reigning with Jesus and pulling down thrones of darkness of this day.

ONLY those who left their baggage behind could cross over into the third day glory, who graduated as kings where their hearts were wholly following the Lord for His purposes to be fulfilled. The Lord promises that we, the sons of God will see a manifestation of His glory. Those who will truly cross over letting everything 'go' represent 'the sons of God' who are entering a type of 'GRADUATION AS KINGS INTO THE THIRD DAY GLORY'.

This is the kairos time for the kings of the earth to prepare for the war of the kings who will bring down thrones of darkness in the earth. God wants to release HIS PRESENT DAY KINGS, but we've got to let go of our present day baggage so that we can cross over to the other side. The Lord showed me that not everyone will go there!! ONLY those that will let go of their baggage, to follow the Lord will cross over to the other side. Yes, God is casting a new mantle on the Ekklesia, and we've got to get ready as the Kings of the Third Day. For you to understand the Third day Church, lets unpack some third day patterns found in scripture.

Revelation of the Third Day Church

According to God's prophetic timetable, we are in the 3rd day of Christ and the 7th day of God. The third day represents 3000 years since Christ's death and the 7th day of God represents 7000 years since creation. They are both the same.

2 Peter 3:8 says, "But do not let this one fact escape your notice, beloved, that with the Lord one day is like a thousand years, and a thousand years like one day." The third day simply represents a 3000 year period since Christ death, and His resurrection.

The Resurrection of Jesus

The earthly ministry of Jesus Christ was concluded on the third day, which we know as the Resurrection Day. The body of Jesus was put in the tomb, and on the third day He arose out of the grave. Resurrection power exploded on the third day when He came up out of the grave and went into Hades taking the keys of victory from the enemy and giving them over to the third day church.

The Third Day Prophetic pattern's in God's Word through Jesus

The ministry of Jesus began on a third day when Jesus changed the water into wine at the wedding of Cana where His first miracle began. John 2:1 -11 says, "On the third day there was a wedding in Cana of Galilee, and the mother of Jesus was there; and both Jesus and His disciples were invited to the wedding. When the wine ran out, the mother of Jesus *said to Him, "They have no wine." And Jesus *said to her, "Woman, what does that have to do with us? My hour has not yet come." His mother *said to the servants, "Whatever He says to you, do it." Now there were six stone water-pots set there for the Jewish custom of purification, containing twenty or thirty gallons each. Jesus *said to them, "Fill the water-pots with water." So they filled them up to the brim. And He *said to them, "Draw some out now and take it to the headwaiter." So they took it to him. When the headwaiter tasted the water which had become wine, and did not know where it came from (but the servants who had drawn the water knew), the headwaiter *called the bridegroom, and *said to him, "Every man serves the good wine first, and when the people have drunk freely, then he serves the poorer wine; but you have kept the good wine until now." This beginning of His signs Jesus did in Cana of Galilee, and manifested His glory, and His disciples believed in Him."

The Best Wine is Reserved for the End of the Church Age

We can also see by this picture that the best wine will be reserved for the end of the Church Age, similar to how the BEST WINE was reserved at the Wedding of Cana. We are the new wineskins that God wants to pour HIS NEW WINE through, but if we're still in an old wineskin mindset, we can't hold the new wine He wants to pour through us.

The way old wineskins were prepared into new wineskins, is they were stretched and then they would soak them in oil so there would be an elasticity and some flexibility in them. Wineskins were used as containers, to hold the new wine. But if they filled the old wineskin with the new wine, before the stretching process the wine would ferment and then burst the old wineskin. Matthew 9:17 says, "Nor do people put new wine into old wineskins; otherwise the wineskins burst, and the wine pours out and the wineskins are ruined; but they put new wine into fresh wineskins, and both are preserved." Therefore when God wants to teach us new things, He has to scrape out the old residue out of us, so He can do something brand new and He will stretch us and pull us into places we're unfamiliar with in order to fill us with the new wine of His Spirit. So allow God to do that. He's waiting on your submission to His leading.

The Third Day Wineskins

The NEW WINE represents the third day wineskins. God wants to scrape out our second day revelation (in the old wineskin) and allow Him to convert our new wineskin into the third day revelation, changing the water into wine, like He did at the wedding of Cana in John 2:1-11. When we do, we're going to experience His resurrection power and see explosions of miracles. Notice that the third day points to a wedding feast. Prophetically I believe we can expect the wedding feasts of Jesus and His Bride to take place on the third day.

Also notice that John 2: 6 says, "Now there were six stone water-pots set there for the Jewish custom of purification, containing twenty or thirty gallons each." Those six stone water pots represent man (6 is the number of man) who was created on the 6th day. (Genesis 1:26-31)

The Servants filled the Six Water Pots

Jesus had the servants fill the six water pots with water, which is a type of the Holy Spirit, and then He changed the water into wine which represents the new wine converting into new revelation into God's people.

Therefore by the power of the Holy Spirit, Jesus takes away the stony heart of man and gives us a heart of flesh that would love Him and walk in His power. Ezekiel 1:19 -20 says, "And I will give them one heart, and put a new spirit within them. And I will take the heart of stone out of their flesh and give them a heart of flesh, that they may walk in My statutes and keep My ordinances and do them. Then they will be My people, and I shall be their God."

Lazarus (John 11: 1-6)

Another Third Day Prophetic Pattern hidden in the scriptures that reveals the power of the Third Day

Church is found in John 11 in the account of Lazarus being raised from the dead.

Lazarus is a picture of those who have been called out of 'DEAD RELIGION' because they're hungry for more. 'Lazarus' name means 'without help.' Therefore we can certainly see without the supernatural power of God, we are without help.

John 11: 1-6 says, "Now a certain man was sick, Lazarus of Bethany, the village of Mary and her sister Martha. It was the Mary who anointed the Lord with ointment, and wiped His feet with her hair, whose brother Lazarus was sick. So the sisters sent word to Him, saying, "Lord, behold, he whom You love is sick." But when Jesus heard this, He said, "This sickness is not to end in death, but for the glory of God, so that the Son of God may be glorified by it."

Now Jesus loved Martha, her sister and Lazarus. Verse 6 says when Jesus heard that Lazarus was sick, He purposely waited two days longer in the place where He was. John 11: 17, 21-23 says, "So when Jesus came, He found he had already been in the tomb four days. Martha was really upset with Jesus. Martha said to Jesus, "Lord, if You had been here, my brother would not have died. Even now I know that whatever You ask of God, God will give You." Jesus *said to her, "Your brother will rise again." Martha *said to Him, "I know he will rise again in the resurrection on the last day."

To the people mourning, it looked like it was over for Lazarus. To the natural mind, 'four days dead' means, "You are too late, Jesus!" However, it was not too late, according to Jesus. He purposely waited to prove this point.

Jesus told Martha in John 11:25 -26, "I am the resurrection and the life; he who believes in Me will live even if he dies, and everyone who lives and believes in Me will never die. Do you believe this?"

Then Jesus commanded Lazarus to come forth. The man who had died came forth, bound hand and foot with wrappings, and his face was wrapped around with a cloth. Jesus *said to them, "Loose him, and let him go."

Guess what? Lazarus came forth at Jesus' command but He still had a veil that covered his face when he came out of the grave. This shows us we can be saved but still bound in our thoughts. We can still have grave clothes on our thinking, bound by unbelief, religion and tradition. Though saved, so to speak, he had a veil over his eyes and he could not move freely.

These miracles point to the Third Day Church coming forth in resurrection power. The Third Day of Christ, in our day, is to be one who shows His resurrection power and demonstrates it to others. That's the power that raised Lazarus from the dead; and that same power dwells in us.

Romans 8:11 says, "But if the Spirit of Him who raised Jesus from the dead dwells in you, He who raised Christ Jesus from the dead will also give life to your mortal bodies through His Spirit who dwells in you."

The Third Day Church is called to loose others from their bondages and bring them into the glorious liberty of the third day. To make this point, He raises up Lazarus from the dead. It's interesting Jesus did not raise Lazarus on the third day; instead He raised Lazarus on the 4th day. Therefore, here the number four represents the ministry that God wants to do through man. Three is the number of the Trinity, plus one for man.

The Traditional Church

We don't know what caused Lazarus to die but we do know that the chief religious leaders wanted to kill both Jesus and Lazarus after Jesus raised him from the dead. The traditional church can become like these same religious Pharisees. The religious leaders tried to put to death those raised up from a dead religion. They had secret plans to kill not only Jesus, but Lazarus too! John 12:9-11 says, "The large crowd of the Jews then learned that He was there; and they came, not for Jesus' sake only, but that they might also see Lazarus, whom He raised from the dead. But the chief priests planned to put Lazarus to death also; because on account of him many of the Jews were going away and were believing in Jesus."

The religious Jews did not want people to believe in Jesus. They tried to oppose what God was doing and they catered to the admiration of men more than the truth of what the miracle meant. In Luke 16:15-16, Jesus was saying to the religious Pharisees, "Now the Pharisees, who were lovers of money, were listening to all these things and were ridiculing Him. And He said to them, "You are the ones who justify yourselves in the sight of people, but God knows your hearts; because that which is highly esteemed among people is detestable in the sight of God."

We're seeing a lot of exposure in this hour of religious Pharisees who clash with the third day kings; always wanting to put them to death. We see here that religious people clash with those that move through the power of the Holy Spirit. The flesh and the Spirit have always clashed because they are from opposite kingdoms.

A Prophetic Alert

God wants us to stand out from those that have tried to block the supernatural power of God. Some of the church has become like the religious Pharisees, and that's why they are without help if they aren't operating on the supernatural power of God; therefore if there's no demonstration of the supernatural power of God, there will be no miracles!

If all you see is religious performance. Please be forewarned they are being exposed, and it grieves the heart of God to see them operate in such deception.

The Mount of Transfiguration

Another Third Day Prophetic Pattern hidden in the scriptures that reveals the power of the Third Day Church is found in Matthew 17 known as the Mount of Transfiguration. Jesus took Peter, James and John up the mountain to reveal the glory of God to them, and they watched Jesus transform right before their eyes.

Matthew 17: 1- 8 says, Jesus *took Peter and James and John and *led them up on a high mountain by themselves. And He was transfigured before them; and His face shone like the sun, and His garments became as white as light. And behold, Moses and Elijah appeared to them, talking with Him. Peter said to Jesus, "Lord, it is good for us to be here; if You wish, I will make three tabernacles here, one for You, and one for Moses, and one for Elijah." While he was speaking, a bright cloud overshadowed them, and behold, a voice out of the cloud said, "This is My beloved Son, with whom I am well-pleased; listen to Him!" When the disciples heard this, they fell face down to the ground and were terrified. And Jesus came to them and touched them and said, "Get up, and do not be afraid. **And lifting up their eyes, they saw no one except Jesus Himself alone."**

Take note of Matthew 17:8 that says, "And lifting up their eyes, they saw no one except Jesus Himself alone." This is why it's crucial for the Third Day Church to keep our eyes on Jesus and Him alone, if we want to see transfiguration in our life, as well as protection. We can't allow anything to hinder our vision of Jesus.

The Third Day Church will receive a Revelation of Jesus Christ

Jesus took three disciples, Peter, James and John who represent the Third Day Church, where they received a revelation of Jesus Christ. This revelation of JESUS was so overwhelming to Peter that with joy he said, "Lord, it is good for us to be here; if You wish, let us make here three tabernacles: one for **YOU**, one for **Moses** and one for **Elijah**."

On the Mount of transfiguration, **Moses** represents the mantle of the **priest**, **Elijah** represents the mantle of the **prophet** and **Jesus** represents the mantle of the **king**. In scripture Jesus was mantled with all three; PRIESTS, PROPHET, and KING.

Each mantle portrayed a heavenly realm of God's glory that will be mantled on the Third Day Church. This is relevant knowing we can't operate in the supernatural without **all three mantles.**

Therefore, God is taking the Third Day Church to a place where we have never been before. But to get there we will have to climb up the mountain just like the disciples did, to get A HEAVENLY VIEW OF JESUS!!! And when we do, the mantles will manifest on us from a heavenly realm all because of JESUS.

The Ezekiel Pattern; The Four Faces of God (Ezekiel 1: 15-28)

Another Third Day Prophetic Pattern hidden in the scriptures that reveals the Third Day Church is found in the first chapter of Ezekiel. The prophet Ezekiel describes a vision he had of 'the four living creatures' faces that point to the attributes of JESUS that are found in the four gospels as well.

The Four Gospels Reveal the following:

- **Matthew** reveals the Lion face of Jesus as our **King**. (This face linked Jesus as the Lion from the Tribe of Judah)

- **Mark** reveals the Man face of Jesus as our **Servant**. (This face linked Him to Son of man)

- **Luke** reveals the Ox face of Jesus as our **Sacrifice**. (This face linked Him to the Son of God)

- **John** reveals the Eagle face of Jesus as our **Destiny**. (This face linked Him to His Destiny)

The **Lion face** represents a kingly anointing that transforms a believer into a king and priest unto God. As we exhibit the lion in the earth, it leads to the **man's face** where we become a bondservant unto God. This leads us into the **ox face** where our sacrifice is given to God, which leads us into the **eagle face** that leads us to soar into our destiny.

We can certainly identify a pattern in Ezekiel through these four faces because they represent the TRUE MATURE SONS OF GOD. If the True sons of God are going to operate in the supernatural, it will be the result of supernatural encounters with Jesus, and the result will cause us to look like Jesus.

Isaiah saw these same four faces on the Seraphim angels as they flew around the throne of God. (Isaiah 6:1-8) The reason the Seraphim angels had the same four faces that Ezekiel saw was because of their proximity to the presence of God. They were so close to the throne of God; they took on the same resemblance of God. This is interesting because it reveals an amazing truth of how worship transforms us to look like Jesus.

The word Seraphim means 'to burn' revealing that when we worship our king, the love of God burns in our heart and we are transformed into Christ's likeness from glory to glory. 2 Corinthians 3:16-18 says, "...but whenever someone turns to the Lord, the veil is taken away. Now the Lord is the Spirit, and where the Spirit of the Lord is, there is freedom. But we all, with unveiled faces, looking as in a mirror at the glory of the Lord, are being transformed into the same image from glory to glory, just as from the Lord..."

Therefore, just like the Seraphim angels that transformed into those four faces, we see clearly from this picture; our worship transforms us into the image of Christ from glory to glory or from one stage of maturity to another.

The Ekklesia is likened to A Wheel Within A Wheel

Ezekiel saw these same four faces. Ezekiel 1:10-14 says, "As for the form of their faces in the middle of the wheels, each had a **human face**; all four had the face of a **lion** on the right and the face of an **ox** on the left, and all four had the face of an **eagle**. Such were their faces. They spread out their wings above; each had two touching another being, and two covering their bodies. And each went straight forward; wherever the spirit was about to go, they would go, without turning as they went."

The creatures do not follow the wheels, but the wheels follow the creatures. (1:19 -21) When the creatures move, the wheels move. When the creatures stopped, the wheels stopped. When the creatures are lifted up, the wheels are lifted up.

This is meaningful. This is in contrast to Christianity's concept, which teaches people to wait upon the Lord till He moves and then they can move. God is awakening us to His movement because we live in Him, and we move in Him. Acts 17: 28 a says, "In Him we live and move and have our being."

The wheel lives upon the breath of the Spirit's coordination; joined to Christ as they are ONE IN HIM WHO MOVES IN SYNC with the Father and the Son. So, it's really both; The Lord follows us, and we follow the Spirit, and the Spirit is in the wheels, because we live on HIS BREATHE! This means we must have a God-confidence, the full assurance, and the faith to move boldly as one being. 1 John 5:14 says, "This is the confidence which we have before Him, that, if we ask anything according to His will, He hears us."

If we move in God's confidence, and in His identity the wheels will turn the axle and the Spirit will lead us. It's not independent but is interdependent on the Spirit because we're ONE WITH HIM.

That lines up with Jesus who did ONLY what He saw His Father do; (John 5:19) therefore our movement is His movement.

A Wheel within a Wheel

As the corporate NEW MAN begins to manifest the Ekklesia will move in greater unity than we have ever known before as ONE BODY fitted together moving by the Spirit. Therefore, when the life of the Ekklesia is tightly woven to the Father's heart; our inner man moves with the Spirit of God as the wheel within the wheel.

In Ezekiel's vision, we see the creatures moved with each spoke of the wheel because they moved by the Spirit. Every wheel relied on the AXLE which turned the wheels. If the axle stopped, the wheels stopped. While we're moving, the Lord is moving in our moving. The axle is **the little wheel within the wheel.** The big wheel turns because the little wheel is being turned by the Spirit. Ezekiel 1:12 says, "And each went **straight forward**; wherever the Spirit was about to go, they would go, without turning as they went." The word **'Straight forward'** in Hebrew #2266 Strong's Concordance comes from the root word **'to cross over'** which can also be rendered **'crossing over with a straight and unchanging purpose.'** In other words, straight is defined as **'moving uniformly in one direction only; without a curve or a bend.'** Scripturally, a curve or a bend represents a propensity toward iniquity. This reveals the corporate third day church will not have a bend toward iniquity because they aren't bound up anymore, and their moving in corporate unity and freedom.

The Example of Wheels on an Axle

As we look at an example of an Axle on a vehicle that makes the wheels turn; Ezekiel 1:16 becomes more real; Ezekiel saw a wheel in the middle of a wheel. This is incredibly significant. When we speak of a whole component of a vehicle, we say that the whole circumference of the vehicle is the engine, the wheels, the axle, the rim, and the spokes. Since we know the axle is the center shaft that rotated the wheels on a vehicle, we are going to parallel the Corporate New Man to an axle that moves a vehicle to its destination.

There are only 2 basic types of automobile axles: the drive axle and a dead axle. The engine itself helps turn the axle. The other type of axle is the dead axle which is not connected to the engine at all. However, when the vehicle is in motion, dead axles are present in every vehicle to help support the weight of the vehicle and the cargo inside of it.

Since the axle is constantly rotating and flexing itself to accommodate different road conditions; if it is not a well-oiled axle; it can wear out. Therefore, using this example we must stay in sync with THE NEW

CORPORATE MAN to carry the weight of THE LORD'S GLORY.

Ephesians 4:2 says, "And be renewed in the spirit of your mind; And that ye **put on the new man**, which after God is created in righteousness and true holiness."

The Dead Axle of Man- made Religion

Do you want to get caught up in the traditions of man spinning around the dead axle of manmade religion, or do you want to move with the corporate anointing as ONE NEW MAN to see the supernatural power of God where miracles will manifest. The answer from all of us should be a simple yes; the promise of "One New Man" is revelatory as we're each properly joined to Christ living in the center of Sonship to please the Father, we will carry the vision as we're tightly woven to His heart.

One New Man in Christ

In the fivefold ascension gifts that are listed in Ephesians 4, we are each connected to Christ; therefore, we should move together as ONE UNIFIED WHEEL. As we step into the fullness of Christ: we're not threatened or in competition with each other; and we should certainly not be jealous of each other.

The Third Day Church is so interwoven with the Father's heart that we're crossing over into unfamiliar territory. This is the Lord's move today on the earth; this is the Lord's recovery and restoration in the land. We're crossing over as ONE CORPORATE NEW MAN who is so intertwined with Him; being one with His purpose.

The Ekklesia

As we stand on the mountaintop to do God's work, we are not alone. God has created an army of people to work together to come against the powers of darkness. We're being given divine favor, but it isn't something we have to work for, but something He assigns to His faithful remnant, through His abundant grace.

The Ekklesia is moving together as One Corporate Body. We know we are stronger together and we should operate to bring balance, expression, integrity, and stability to arrive at our destination. Therefore, we see clearly in the scriptures, we cannot win the corporate battle until the FULL STATURE OF CHRIST IS SEEN IN THE CORPORATE MATURE SON.

As we move in unity together corporately, we're going to resemble the TRUE MATURE SONS OF GOD. The evidence of our maturity should align us together as ONE NEW MAN. Yes, for sure, the Ekklesia will exhibit JESUS IN THE EARTH, Christ in us the hope of glory. (Colossians 1:17) We are all being conformed into His image day by day into the image of God's beloved Son. Paul writes, in Romans 8: 29 saying, "For those He foreknew, He also predestined to be conformed to the image of His Son, that He might be the firstborn among many brothers."

These signs of supernatural power and glory will manifest in the true Ekklesia (a remnant or a company of people) who are called out of this world's system. The Greek word for Ekklesia represents 'a company being called out' and as stated before in an earlier chapter this refers to something different from the church that meets in a building. Let's reiterate one more time what Ekklesia means: The Latin word for 'called out' is Ecclesia, but the Greek word for Ekklesia is a compound of two words: 'ek', which is a preposition meaning 'out of', and the verb, 'kaleo', signifying 'to call' and then put the two words together, and it literally means, 'to call out of'.

Jesus said, "I will build MY EKKLESIA and the gates of Hell will not prevail against it." (Matthew 16:18b)

God is going to restore The Third Day Church; and deliver many that will yield in this new season. However, many that won't yield are about to fall.

We need to rejoice; because it's a chosen position planned by God that will manifest many miracles. And strategically, we're at the tipping point for the most magnificent end time move the earth has ever seen.

The Three Heavens

This may not seem revelent to what we're talking about but there's a need to teach on the three heavens.

In 2 Corinthians 12:1-2, Paul speaks of three heavens.

1) The first heaven is what we see with our natural eyes.

2) The second heaven is where principalities, powers and wickedness in heavenly places are.

Remember the teaching on Jezebel as a Principality in the previous chapter.

3) The third heaven is where God dwells with His angelic host. Therefore, in order to paralyze principalities and Satan and his acts in the second heaven, the Ekklesia must move together corporately in unity.

The power of agreement is the key to spiritual alignment, giving us the power to paralyze the enemy in spiritual high places. Yet our division in the first heaven means we are not operating in Kingdom authority to deactivate principalities in the second heaven. As we become ONE NEW MAN IN CHRIST, we will deactivate principalities and the powers of darkness through our unity. It is just a matter of readjusting our agreement.

Jesus said in, "Truly I say to you, whatever you bind on earth shall have been bound in heaven; and whatever you loose on earth shall have been loosed in heaven. Again, I say to you, that if two of you agree on earth about anything that they may ask, it shall be done for them by My Father who is in heaven. For where two or three have gathered together in My name, I am there in their midst." (Matthew 18:18-20) The Greek text says, "I am there to make good that which they agree on." (Matthew 18:20)

We see clearly in the scriptures; we cannot win the corporate battle without being One NEW Man in Christ! The reason we benefit from being fitted and held together is that every joint supplies its individual purpose, making movement in the Spirit and being effective in doing the work of the ministry.

This is how the complete body increases and prospers, because we can do more together than apart. God requires inter-dependence throughout the body of Christ meaning we need to move as One together. No one person has all the anointing, all the revelation, all the gifts, or all the power. Therefore, in order for us to get all that is available to us, we have to receive from others and accept their ministry, calling and anointing.

Ephesians 4: 11-16 that says, "And He gave some as apostles, and some as prophets, and some as evangelists, and some as pastors and teachers, for the equipping of the saints for the work of service, to

313

the building up of the body of Christ; until we all attain to the unity of the faith, and of the knowledge of the Son of God, to a mature man, to the full measure of the stature which belongs to the fullness of Christ. As a result, we are no longer to be children, tossed here and there by waves and carried about by every wind of doctrine, by the trickery of men, by craftiness in deceitful scheming; but speaking the truth in love, we are to grow up in all aspects into Him who is the head, even Christ, from whom the whole body, being fitted and held together by what every joint supplies, according to the proper working of each individual part, causes the growth of the body for the building up of itself in love."

The whole body is fitly joined together so that every joint supplies what we need, making us all effective in doing the work of the ministry.

Psalm 110 is a Prophecy about The Melchizedek Priestly/ Kingly Order

Psalm 110 speaks of a day that God's power will manifest in the corporate Ekklesia, where she will arise and be victorious. Psalms 110:1-5 says, "The Lord says to my Lord: "Sit at My right hand until I make Your enemies a footstool for Your feet." The Lord will stretch out Your strong scepter from Zion, saying, "Rule in the midst of Your enemies." Your people will volunteer freely on the day of Your power; In holy splendor, **from the womb of the dawn**, Your youth are to You as the dew. The Lord has sworn and will not change His mind, "You are a priest forever according to the **order of Melchizedek.**"

Melchizedek is an interesting title that we do not hear much teaching on. Melchizedek was a title given to Priests and warrior Kings.

What do Priests do? They worship. What do Kings do? They go out to battle and fight, to conquer battles corporately.

GOD IS GOING TO MANIFEST His third day glory through us. We are the true Sons of God ACTIVATING THE KINGDOM AS WE SIT IN HEAVENLY AGREEMENT RULING AND REIGNING WITH JESUS.

The Womb of the Dawn

What does "in Holy Array" mean in Psalm 110:3? Psalm 110: verse 3 says, "**In holy array, from the womb of the dawn,** your youth are to You as the dew. The LORD has sworn and will not change His mind, you are a priest forever **according to the order of Melchizedek.** The Lord is at Your right hand; He will shatter kings in the day of His wrath." Coming out of the womb of the dawn means **APOSTOLIC KINGS** are dressed in Holy array for **corporate warfare** because we know our authority as kings. The '**womb of the dawn**' represents **apostolic warfare being birthed from the corporate womb** of the Ekklesia according to the order of Melchizedek; giving an eviction notice to the enemy and his principalities. Therefore, coming out of the womb of the dawn **in Holy array, represents warriors coming into a life of corporate unity and obedience to the Father**.

Then Psalm 110: 4 says, "The LORD says to my Lord: "**Sit at My right hand UNTIL I make Your enemies a footstool for Your feet." As we rest our feet on the footstool, we are ruling over the enemy. This agreement gives us the power to rule over satanic activity. God will back us up; because it's in the TITLE DEED COMMISSIONING US INTO AN APOSTOLIC WARFARE COMPANY.**

The right hand represents a place of power and authority and resting feet on a footstool as a seated person represents ruling with Jesus through His authority.

When we realize we can rest our feet over the things that the enemy throws at us, and that being seated represents our victory has already been completed on the cross then we are operating in the MIGHTY AUTHORITY of what Jesus has already done. We know we have the 'TITLE DEED' which is the WORD of God and we are reinforcing what's been documented to us as WARRIOR KINGS.

A Wheel with Eyes

Ezekiel saw a wheel within a wheel alongside each, where the rims were filled with eyes. (Ezekiel 1:18) This represents the Body of Christ receiving new revelation from the Spirit of God and moving together through that revelation as ONE.

Ephesians 1:17- 23 says, "that the God of our Lord Jesus Christ, the Father of glory, may give to you a Spirit of wisdom and of revelation in the knowledge of Him. **I pray that the eyes of your heart may be**

enlightened, so that you will know what is the hope of His calling, what are the riches of the glory of His inheritance in the saints, and what is the surpassing greatness of His power toward us who believe. These are in accordance with the working of the strength of His might which He brought about in Christ, when He raised Him from the dead and seated Him at His right hand in the heavenly places, far above all rule and authority and power and dominion, and every name that is named, not in this age but also in the one to come. And He put all things in subjection under His feet, and have Him as head over all things to the church, the fullness of Him who fills all in all."

In the midst of the living beings that Ezekiel saw there was something that looked like burning coals of fire, like torches moving among the living beings. Fire burst forth through these creatures as they moved in new revelation from the throne of God as flashes of lightning. Above their heads was the likeness of a throne with the appearance of sapphire stones, and on the throne high above them was a figure like that of a man. (Ezekiel 1:26)

As they kept their eyes on Jesus, the living beings ran back and forth like bolts of lightning.

The Third Day Church is progressively moving as the true sons of God into a higher dimensions of revelation, as we keep our eyes on Jesus as well. We're the kings of the Third Day who will receive a revelation of Jesus who are being empowered to see the thrones of darkness thrown down. God is about to give the Ekklesia a third day mantle that will release many powerful miracles and deep mysteries of God are being released for this season.

The Lord is creating a company of kings in the earth to manifest the true sons of God, and all creation is groaning for it (Romans 8:19). This company of third day kings are being gathered together to establish GOD's purpose. They WILL COME TOGETHER as a resounding voice to break off the strongholds of resistance that are against THE KINGDOM OF GOD. God is calling the true sons of God to arise corporately as a remnant to manifest A KINGDOM REVOLUTION. God is calling radical revolutionists to be His Paul Revere's. Therefore arise sons of God; for you were born for such a time as this!

Conclusion

Birthing the True Sons of God in the Earth

As we are marinating in the Spirit of glory, we are going to suffer for the Lord, but when we do, we are to rejoice because to the degree that we share in the sufferings of Christ, is the degree that we will share in HIS GLORY. Therefore, we count it ALL JOY when we suffer for His Name's sake.

The Apostle Peter said in 1 Peter 4:7, "**The end of all things is near**; therefore, be of sound judgment and sober spirit for the purpose of prayer." The word 'sober' in the Greek is 'sophroneo' and it means to be awakened, to watch and be alert. The definition is i.e. (1) to be awakened (2) to be watchful (3) to be alert, (4) to be of sound mind, (5) to be temperate, (6) to have sound judgment (7), a right mind (8), and to be sensible.

When Peter goes on to say here in this passage when he said, "The end of all things is near." This doesn't mean the end of the world, even though eventually that will happen, but rather the end of things as we know it. It's the end of an administration or the start of a transition. Then the Apostle Peter added 1 Peter 4:12, saying, "Beloved, do not be surprised at the fiery ordeal among you, which comes upon you for your testing, as though some strange thing were happening to you; but to the degree that you share the sufferings of Christ, keep on rejoicing, so that also at the revelation of His glory you may rejoice with exultation. If you are reviled for the Name of Christ, you are blessed, because the Spirit of glory and of God rests on you."

Many of God's people are coming around full circle. This full circle means you're standing at the point of your original beginning. It's a refreshing place, but the reason it's being restored is that now we're MORE FULLY SURRENDERED TO THE LORD and we're being prepared to step into God's ordained plan.

God is bringing HIS PEOPLE full circle to a place of origin to let US begin again without reproach because the suffering we went through brought us into full maturity and a greater depth of power that now we can steward the blessing in a greater capacity.

We've been brought full circle; this process has qualified MANY TO RECEIVE THE REWARDS OF OUR

JOURNEY, AND IT IS ALLOWING NEW FREEDOM from those things that are behind us. The tests that we have endured have prepared us to be stronger.

This NEW strength and clarity will serve us well in our spiritual progression. This place of reproach has brought us into full-grown maturity and has given us a special grace that we've stepped into because it's a PREPARED PLACE.

There is a remnant being called out of another remnant. Those who have been wounded are called back in the fight with new strategies; and there won't be a trace of a scar found on you.

What you thought was dead has only been resting in the wilderness, growing and developing. God is about to emerge many from a place of dark seclusion. As much as you have tried to not be hidden or private, God has used this time to bring a much needed healing. That place of silence has been necessary to your spiritual, emotional, mental and physical well-being. However, things are about to change. Prepare yourself to be brought forth into the light of a higher place where you will understand the revelation and the purpose of your seclusion.

We are GLORY CARRIERS AS TRUE SONS OF GOD. Therefore, the GLORY is the power that transforms our existence into a true son of God. And even a greater truth; it belongs to GOD's people.

Let's partner with God, and He will multiply our resources, our strength, and our ability to overcome many things that have hindered us before. When we allow God to fill our beings, our homes, our families, our lives, our churches, our ministries, and our nation with the glory of God we will see transformation. Lord, let Your Glory change us, and wash through our nation and shine Your glory through us as THE TRUE SONS OF GOD TO REVEAL A KINGDOM REVOLUTION IN OUR LIVES AND IN THE EARTH WHEREVER WE GO!

Prophetess Bonjie Wernecke Rodriguez

Author, Founder & Director

Door of Hope Inner Healing & Deliverance School

Prophetess Bonjie Rodriguez has been in ministry for over 36 years. In 2004 she graduated with a Bachelor Degree from Calvary Theological Seminary that is based in Lake Charles, Louisiana. She is an ordained minister, Author of 4 Books, Conference Speaker, Prophetess, A Prophetic Teacher, Apostolic Mentor that has raised up many Sons and Daughters . She teaches people how to connect in intimacy to God, rather than through performance and working for approval; and how to change from being an orphan to being an heir in THE KINGDOM of GOD.

Bonjie Wernecke Rodriguez is Founder and Director of Door of Hope Inner Healing and Deliverance School since 2008. Her ministry is to awaken sons and daughters and connect them to their purpose and calling to perpetuate them into their GENERATIONAL BLESSINGS IN THE KINGDOM of God. She has ministered in prisons, school campuses, and rehabilitation hospitals as well as giving herself to the homeless. She has been interviewed on Houston's local Daystar Broadcasting Network and on many radio station interviews.

God transformed Bonjie's life in 1982 where she was emotionally wounded and was very shame- based that she became suicidal; but God sent a powerful intercessor who became a spiritual mother to her that led her into recovery and a deep relationship with the Lord. God propelled her into a miraculous journey only led by Him.

Door of Hope Inner Healing and Deliverance Classes has ran classes from 2008- to the present. She saw many wounded people healed from the inside out miraculously by the power of God. Bonjie has the heart to see the church come into her fullness of healing. She moves strongly in the gifts of the prophetic, accompanied by a strong healing ministry. Bonjie has a love for the bride to see her raised up equipped, and walking in the gifts and teaching the body of

Christ how to overcome through knowing their identity in Christ. Having many personal testimonies of life altering events and walking the pathway to restoration and recovery, she believes all things are possible with God. God gave her a vision of an Inner Healing and Deliverance School based upon her journey where she wrote a 21 Week DOH Mentoring Course. The Mentoring Course offers a Book, A Teaching Manual and a Workbook that are designed to reach out to these types of needs:

Depression, Shame and Guilt

Toxic Relationships

Addictions

Phobias, Terror and Panic Attacks

Chaotic Lifestyle

Isolation

Insecurity

Orphan Traits

Inability to Trust

Rage Attacks

Emotional, Physical, and Sexual Abuse

Loss through Death, Divorce & Abortion

Suicidal feelings

No purpose in life

Bonjie has recently published her Book: Kingdom Revolution: Birthing the True Sons of God in the Earth released on Amazon.com. This Book has ignited the power of God to see people's lives revolutionized. Bonjie has started KINGDOM REVOLUTION TEACHINGS AND CONFERENCES TO OVERTHROW AN OLD WAY OF THINKING INTO A BRAND-NEW WAY. Therefore, as we stand in our kingdom liberty, we are a part of that KINGDOM REVOLUTION that never returns to the 'OLD WAY OF THINKING' but allows the Spirit of God to completely revolutionize us!

Visit our website-www.mydoorofhopeministries.org – to find all her mentoring tools. To find out how to invite Bonjie to speaking engagements; or, how to invite her to your church to start a Door of Hope Mentoring Class or for ministry services, please contact Bonjie personally at: hope@mydoorofhopeministries.org or Bonjie@MyDoorOfHopeMinistries.org

Made in the USA
Coppell, TX
17 August 2022

81650395R00184